Embodied
CREATION

The sensitive's way
to consciously co-create

TARA JACKSON

ISBN:
978-1-913590-52-9 (Paperback)
978-1-913590-53-6 (ebook)

Cover design by Lynda Mangoro.
Cover photograph by Brendan Jackson.

The Unbound Press
www.theunboundpress.com

Hey unbound one!

Welcome to this magical book brought to you by The Unbound Press.

At The Unbound Press we believe that when women write freely from the fullest expression of who they are, it can't help but activate a feeling of deep connection and transformation in others. When we come together, we become more and we're changing the world, one book at a time!

This book has been carefully crafted by both the author and publisher with the intention of inspiring you to move ever more deeply into who you truly are.

We hope that this book helps you to connect with your Unbound Self and that you feel called to pass it on to others who want to live a more fully expressed life.

With much love,

Nicola Humber

Founder of The Unbound Press
www.theunboundpress.com

KIND WORDS ABOUT EMBODIED CREATION

In *Embodied Creation* Tara Jackson somehow manages to describe the indescribable - the mysterious, magical process that enables us to bring our desires and creations into form. Whether you're working on a creative project or wanting to create a particular change in your life, this book will act as both a powerful guide and activation. Thank you Tara for bringing through this manifesto for creating in a new and soul-aligned way!.
Nicola Humber, Founder of The Unbound Press & Transformational Writing Mentor,
www.theunboundpress.com.

I feel like I drank in the wisdom contained within *Embodied Creation* and it was only after I'd finished reading it, I realised just how thirsty I'd been for this work. Tara's writing is beautiful and lyrical, and her words sink deeply into the body as well as the mind. Her insights and guidance are inspiring and empowering – I feel excited about creating again, and about the possibilities of doing this as a co-creation with (and for) something greater than just me. Thank you for offering this to us, Tara. I know that many more creations will be brought to life thanks to the power of *Embodied Creation*.
Anna Sansom, Writer & Desire Line Walker,
www.annasansom.com.

Every word within *Embodied Creation* feels like coming home to truth. Feel every cell in your body relax as you melt into your divine feminine knowing and permission to become the creator you already are, no pushing, no trying, no chasing. Tara's book merges ancient wisdom, intuitive knowing and modern day lived experience, allowing you to reignite a deep sense of trust in the creation process and yourself. This is not a book to be read, it's a book to be felt and embodied. Flowing with yourself and the energies you're co-creating with.
Debra Kilby, Energy Healer, Intuitive Guide, Baby Spirit Communicator and Channel for Spirit, www.debrakilby.com.

Embodied Creation is powerful. Timely. The world needs these words at this moment. It is the antithesis to so much we have been taught, ringing with truth, resonating with our deep inner knowing. I love the pace, the inclusion of poetry, prose, questions, and vulnerability.

Both gentle and wild, you have given words to the intangible, created a guide and framework to embody inner work.

Words fail me - in actuality - to tell you exactly how abundantly I enjoyed Embodied Creation. As I read I felt my soul rise up in agreement, click into alignment, inhale and deeply exhale. Each section was affirming, confirming, and inspiring - I am so grateful. Thank you. Thank you. Thank you.

Angel Ludwig, Organisational Design Consultant, www.paceofpeople.com.

This book is deeply layered. Right from the get-go, it is clear that Tara is on a mission. Her kind words validate the journey of sensitive souls who desire to create a more sustainable way of living and connect to others differently. She offers practical and intuitive guidance for stepping into our roles as co-creators with the Earth.

I love how she weaves the seasons and the chakras into working with and honouring our own inner cycles. This book opens you to purpose but with child-like abandon, fuelled by wonder and curiosity.

Aparna Vemula, Intuitive Coach, Usui Reiki Master and Soul Realignment™ Practitioner, www.whisperwithin.me.

An inspiring book for sensitive creatives and much needed for Earth's ascension!

In *Embodied Creation - The sensitive's way to consciously co-create*, Tara offers a new paradigm shift towards creativity and manifestation, without the spiritual manifestation mainstream fluff that we see today. This is a real and raw depiction of how creativity should be approached; respecting Mother Gaia, Her seasons, as well as the human's cycles, with examples of real people and practical tips such as the journaling prompts and actionable tasks.

I recommend this wonderful soulful creation to all creative empaths, artists, entrepreneurs, and anyone who wants to follow a more creative spiritual path within. This is also perfect to all of

those who have the intention to co-create in sustainable ways for the highest good of the collective. Tara reminds us that the power to heal the world lies within each and every one of us and that we are always guided and provided for.
Will Caminada, Spirit Guide, Singer-Songwriter, Author, www.willcaminada.com.

With her new book *Embodied Creation*, Tara Jackson guides her reader on a spiralling journey home to the cyclical wisdom of the body and the Earth. She calls us to co-create a world that honours nature and all life, showing us how it all begins by nurturing and listening to the vessel for our creations, our bodies. There is a wealth of prompts, practices and enquiries to help make the exploration of co-creation an embodied experience, and to support us in meeting and moving through the blocks that may arise along the way. The book names and challenges the patriarchal, consumerist principles that have driven our planet into climate crisis and fostered devastating inequality within society. The power of the Feminine sings through Tara's words as she invites us to restore balance to our hyper-masculine culture. Embodied Creation is a passionate, insightful and inspiring book. I am sure that I will be returning to it again and again as I navigate my own creative journey.
Rosalie Kohler, Artist, Writer and Yoga Nidra Facilitator, www.spiralshores.com.

In a world that is always 'on' Tara brings us back to our deep knowing and intuition, encouraging us to connect to the beat of our heart and the rhythm of our soul, to tap into the inner wisdom that we all hold within, but have become so detached from; to get out of our head and into our body, to stop pushing and striving and let it be easy. A scary prospect? Maybe. But the way she writes resonates: it's so relatable that it feels like common sense, and then she shares her own experiences and shows it's do-able too. Within these pages she invites you to bring your whole self into play: to align your personal, professional and business development, and to trust. I have the utmost respect and admiration for Tara's courage, honesty, insight and commitment to her purpose. This is an author who walks her talk and isn't afraid to share the messiness of life in her quest to bring this powerful approach to the world. If you've read her two earlier books this one won't disappoint. If you're new to her work, you're in for a treat.

Lisa Bove, Executive Coach, www.lisabove.com.

I have been a creative for over 20 years. I have also lived outside of my own body for most of my life. *Embodied Creation* arrived at the exact right moment in my life, and supported me to excavate and see the final piece of the puzzle in my current journey. And that is: in order to create in an embodied way, I have to allow my spirit to fully inhabit my physical body. This means, accepting my body, loving it and nurturing it, exactly as it is, because the guidance from my Higher Self and Spirit, and the souls of my creation, come through the body.

In this book, Tara offers us a step by step process for how to take the seed or spirit of an idea and bring it into the physical world, and, to do so in a way that deeply nourishes us, and nurtures our hearts and bodies. As we do this, we not only create inspired works and impactful businesses, we also create an entirely new way of being and living. Which means, we begin creating a new world.

If you are a highly sensitive person, or, a sensitive soul who is tired of working against yourself, and your own rhythms, this book is the breath of spirit you have been waiting for. Embodied Creation is the deep exhale that returns us to our own breath. It is the gentle voice encouraging us to listen to our heart's whisper, and the warm wind saying: "Yes, you are supported. Show us your light, we are ready for you. We are waiting."

Toni Giselle Stuart, Poet, Performer & Creative Facilitator, www.tonistuart.com.

Embodied Creation is about a courageous and radically different way of creating, aligned with the times we live in. Answering the call of Mother Earth to co-create with her for the good of all of life. I know this book is going to be my midwifery guide as we birth a new way of being, doing and creating.

Karin Huber, Earth Keeper,
www.instagram.com/nourishing_mother_earth.

For mum, whose energy has been with me closer than ever whilst I co-created this book.

I miss you and I love you.

CONTENTS

WHO THIS BOOK IS FOR

This book is for the heart-centred, sensitive, empathic, and creative ones; the ones who feel so much and genuinely care about the whole. For the ones who are here to make a compassionate difference in this world by co-creating with what wants to come through.

As a sensitive soul, you have the gift of feeling the energy, the essence or life-force of people, animals and things acutely. You can feel the energy of spaces, the land, a room after someone has left it, and even inanimate objects. You can feel or just know how others are feeling. You sense what's needed and what's not being said. You are in tune with your body's guidance and messages as the intuitive part of your being.

As a sensitive soul, you care. Deeply. You feel pain. You feel suffering. You feel loss. You feel the unfairness of a world that has become deeply un-balanced under its patriarchal rule. It may have overwhelmed and stopped you in the past, or made you feel like you had to lessen your own greatness and strengths – after all, who are you to have it all when others can barely get by?

This strength of sensitivity is something that I absolutely believe is one of the reasons why you are here.

You are here to lean into your sensitivity, to let it lead and guide you, to support you to vision the new ways that will help heal systems that create more struggle and suffering, to release that which isn't serving, to be a way-shower and above all, to come from the heart and bring more love in.

You are being invited to co-create with what you feel, and what you are being called to bring onto this planet. Deeply aligning with the rhythms nature shows us. You are here to lean into the power of your heart and soul, to let them lead and to truly come from this place, embodying what it means to be one.

It's also about asking for and receiving the guidance available to us, whether that's from others or the unseen, non-physical and other realms. It's about co-creating with others, as we are not meant to – we actually can't – do this alone. To truly create a planet that changes and dismantles systems of oppression and begins to invite in the guidance that will support this new world so many of us are tapping into, we have to do it together.

Above all, you are here to create the new, in a different, magical and original way!

This book is my invitation to you to step into that, if you are feeling that call, my fellow sensitive soul.

EMBODIED CREATION

When I first started writing this book, feeling its energy and letting it guide me, I thought it was going to be purely about manifestation. Creating and bringing what you want/desire/choose to focus on into your life. I was a bit surprised that this is what I would be writing about. Whilst manifestation is a topic I have always been interested in and actively work on in my life weekly, and at times daily, it felt a bit uninspiring to be writing yet a-n-o-t-h-e-r book on the topic. What could I add that was going to be any different from the thousands of books out there on manifesting already? Also, did I really want to write about how to bring in more money, stuff, etc.?

As I committed to the journey of co-creating this book, following the guidance I was given, it took me on a whole other journey and led to something quite different which still connected to manifesting/creating.

The first thing I was guided to do was connect with people globally and share my (hybrid from many teachers) manifesting/creating process to show how creation is for anyone. As I began to have conversations with the magical souls worldwide, I realised that they mostly wanted to create feelings and qualities in their life – more love, connection, presence, happiness, freedom. Sure, some wanted more money and clients, but it was only for the freedom it gave, and the ability to be able to help others more and give back in many ways. There were also some who wanted to create offers through their business and manifest spaces where they could truly make a difference and have a greater impact with the work they are here to do. One even was creating a baby, wanting to do it in a conscious, embodied way.

This was totally in alignment with my heart and soul, and reminded me of my bigger purpose, which is to help create a world which benefits ALL and is in harmony with the natural world. That moves away from vast consumerism feeding the profits of global corporations. Unsustainable over-consumption that is destroying our planet and keeping slave labour and other harmful and degrading industries alive. Practices which promote an individual, survival of the fittest (or the one with the most resources) approach with no consideration for the whole.

So often in manifesting teachings in the west (or at least the majority that I have come across), there's a promoting of unlimited resources for all – handbags, cars, homes, etc. Whilst I absolutely believe in adopting a mindset that enables you to move past scarcity and struggle, there literally are not unlimited resources for all on Earth. We cannot keep taking and pillaging from the Earth and her resources, using cheap labour in countries where there is extreme poverty, to produce this unlimited supply of abundance that is being promoted.

However, I completely understand wanting to and needing to ensure your needs are met, to feel safe and supported. This is what ultimately began my manifesting journey as I was in so much debt and unemployed in my late 20s. It was a struggle to buy food some months, let alone pay rent. I also deeply support money being in the hands of people that will do good with it for the whole.

At the end of the day, we are here on Earth for a short time. To enjoy it, and experience it fully is what being human is all about. But we can't do that if we destroy it. We don't actually own anything (in my opinion) as we can't take anything with us when we leave. So why do we need to hoard it?

We all ultimately want to create and manifest something that brings us a feeling – whether it's joy, love, connection, freedom, etc. And when we do the inner work and healing that the journey of creation invites us on, we may find we don't need as much stuff. It also doesn't give us the feelings we desire long term, or on as deep a level as it does with true human connection and with this planet, I personally don't feel.

There is also a deep shadow side to manifesting that I feel ties into privilege. I am incredibly privileged compared to most. I was adopted into a wealthy (by Kenyan standards – where I grew up) white family, even though I am biologically Indian, so I grew up with that privilege. As a child, I had a private education, and my basic needs were always met, plus I have had opportunities and support available to me throughout my life. Is my privilege a reason I am able to manifest/create some things more easily and quicker than others? I absolutely believe so.

We are all powerful creators, but it's our backgrounds, conditioning, beliefs, stories, circumstances, opportunities, ancestry, education, support, and more that all play a part in how easily we can manifest and create. We've also been conditioned to feel scarcity and lack and, as such, feel like we have to hoard to feel a sense of safety and control.

Ultimately, we need to feel and align with what we want to bring in and take our guided action to co-create. That will likely come more easily to someone who a) has the time to do the inner work and isn't struggling to make ends meet, and b) has the resources and education on where to get support and help.

I also feel that those of us who are in positions of power due to our privilege have a responsibility to do what we can to create for ourselves first and foremost – as this journey has the potential to take you deep inside all of you and heal for the collective and for future generations. But alongside this I feel we need to do it with an *active* intention for the good of all and this planet. This is the piece I feel has been missing from within the boom of manifesting and creating amongst spiritual, and now more mainstream, circles.

This book is that.

It is a call to co-create for the good of the whole. To return to the natural rhythms and cycles of creation, as this is where we can truly create a sustainable future. This is where our creations will thrive as we *remember* we are not machines and need to rest and replenish as well as take action, where we give back as well as receive, where we honour endings as much as beginnings.

It asks you to slow down and go within to align with a way that creates deeply with your body and the planet. A way that honours the role and power of the feminine in creation, alongside the masculine.

As you begin to deeply create from this place, it asks you to get out of your own way and ask the questions: Am I creating from my soul and heart, or my ego? Are you allowing what wants to come through you?

It invites you to co-create with Gaia, her energies, and what is calling to be created at this time, whilst holding and healing what needs to be released and let go, so that you can truly align with what you are here to bring through.

Thank you for walking this path alongside me.
All my love,
Tara

HOW TO USE THIS BOOK

This is a book to support you with conscious co-creation. It will support you to tune into your gifts, your desires, your unique essence and what you are here to embody and bring into the physical, deeply tuning into the wisdom of Mother Earth (who I sometimes refer to as Gaia throughout), and what she is calling for.

It is an 'active' book. It is about using it to support you and following the guidance and prompts within, plus the additional resources listed at the end, and getting external support if you need it.

I recommend reading the 'Foundations' and 'The creation process' sections first, as together they give an overview for the intention of the book, prompts and ways to begin to co-create and support yourself to do this from an embodied place. Within 'The creation process' there is also a sub-section on 'Getting started'. Then there is the 'Creation blocks' section which will support you with any resistance, beliefs or blocks rising on your journey of co-creation.

After this there is the 'Seasons of creation' section, which contains inspiration from nature to guide and remind you to tune into the essence of that season (which I explain more later on), as well as prompts, practices and actions you can take to align with its qualities and connect more deeply with what you are bringing through.

As you begin to consciously co-create something, I invite YOU to trust which section (spring, summer, autumn/fall and winter) is calling you. You could look at the contents page and pick a title that draws you in. You might decide to start in the spring and connect to your vision, or perhaps even winter if you are feeling called to nourish deeply before you begin co-creating. If you are feeling the seasonal energy in the year, you could go for that one. You might want to use the seasons of your menstrual cycle (if applicable) or the moon cycle. There's more on this later. You can ask your creation which season it would like you to lean into.

You might find yourself in one section more than another. You might find you flick about, leaning into some areas more than others. Trust the wisdom of your body as you use this part. In fact, trust the wisdom of your body throughout.

At the end is a section on 'Birthing your creation', with some guidance and prompts on bringing your creation into the physical and what this might be like.

I have to deeply emphasise that this creation process is certainly not linear. I repeat: this process is not linear! It's cyclical, spiralling and can be all over the place – in fact, it can be frustrating and messy as hell!

It's about letting go of any pre-conceived ideas of it fitting a form. Letting your inner wisdom and what you are co-creating with guide you, always trusting what feels right and above all surrendering to YOUR co-creative journey, whilst holding an intention for the highest good of all.

EMBODIED CREATION COMES FROM THE BODY

It seems so obvious, but it took me a while to fully get this! All parts of us – mind, soul and body – have their place, but fundamentally embodied creation is a deep honouring of the body and its inherent ability to create. To feel the energies of what is calling to be created, and to be the co-creator in bringing them into the physical.

Listen to me.
Feel me.
Move with me.
Be still with me.

I am a gift from the Earth.
I am of her.
I carry her wisdom.
I am part of the whole.

I must be nurtured.
I must be nourished.
I must be held.
I must be respected.

I need love.
I need connection.
I need rest.
I need play.

Then together with my messages, my guidance, my signs and my signals,
You will intuit the way.

FOUNDATIONS

This section lays the grounding for *Embodied Creation*, including how I created this book with the energy of it. It shares what the 'Seasons of creation' are, the qualities they generally embody, and how you can use them. It also shares the part the heart plays in creating in this way, and how you can lean into it.

What is Embodied Creation?

Embodied Creation is creation in all forms – creating offers, businesses, a life that feels good, art, music, other physical embodiments of love, and absolutely anything – in alignment with your body and the planet. It deeply acknowledges the Great Mother, our Earth Mother (Gaia), her seasons and cycles that we are naturally created by, born by and are guided to live by. It honours that we are part of the whole, that our bodies are of the Earth.

Creation is a bringing together of the masculine and feminine energies, which we all carry inside us. It is finding this wholeness within, embodying these energies, to create from this space.

It's about coming back into the energy centres of our beings – the chakras – each carrying their own strengths and wisdom, tuning into them to connect back to a place of higher consciousness and a space of wholeness.

It's about collectively creating a world for the greater good of all, not just for a few to thrive at the expense of others and the Earth. It acknowledges the fact that we have created so much separation and division on this planet, that there is much 'work' to be done, and we have to put the needs of the many at the forefront. This has to be integral to creation, it has to come from a deeply embodied place of care and compassion and understanding that we are all in this together.

It's about creating a space where we are all accepted for who we are, where we are equal, where we care for one another, we work together and are there for one another. We know that all our different qualities are needed and the power in that is unfathomable.

It's letting go of the limitations, the stories and beliefs that have been playing out for centuries, keeping us all small and stuck, in patterns which do not serve. It's recognising that there is much deep healing to do around this, releasing of past conditioning and

stepping out of the current patriarchal system which presides.
It's a remembering that we are more powerful than many of us could ever imagine, and now is not the time to abdicate that power. We can, we must, claim it back as our responsibility and use it to co-create a reality in alignment with the unique qualities that we each came here to embody and express, in a way that honours the needs of all, not just a few.

It's also re-claiming your magic, leaning into fun, pleasure and play – reminding yourself that you are here to enjoy life as well.

Above all it's about:
Creating a life that you love.
A life that benefits all.
A life that respects the planet.
A life that feels good from deep within.
A life that you came here for.

You, dear sensitive reader, are a powerful co-creator and it is time.

A letter from Embodied Creation ...

(Asking Her what she would like to share, this is what I received)

Creation is by its nature sustainable when it follows the natural cycle of gestation, growth, death and rebirth.

There is nothing sustainable about promoting the creation of unlimited wealth and resources. It's simply not possible, as it's not being given time to replenish. Creation has become out of hand, excessive, greedy, selfish. We don't need unlimited stuff, things and resources. Look at what we are destroying as we try to satisfy this bottomless pit.

Learning from, living by and going back to our bodies and roots to live in harmony with nature is what we are being called to do. Spending time with people we love, connecting and getting back into the wild – learning from nature's rhythms and other sentient beings.

As creation comes back to this, we begin to co-create with Gaia; we start to honour her, and it goes beyond the individual and considers the whole. We remember our inter-connectedness. We take what we need and give back in abundance. We look after our home and each other, and restore peace, harmony and balance.

As we create from our hearts and souls, we bring ideas forth that care for others, that help and support others to be more of themselves, that create new ways, that come from love and wholeness.

The world needs you to be the most you that you can possibly be, as from this place you align with the highest vision of what you are here to create.

OF THE EARTH

You are the delicate beauty of the cherry blossom in springtime.
The squishy moss-bed on the forest floor.
The mesmerising mystery of the luminescent full moon.
The embodied strength of the sun rising at dawn.
You are the depths of the ocean.
The vastness of the starry night sky.

Your veins mimic the meanders of rivers flowing.
Your lungs the exquisite ecosystem of a lush rainforest.
The contours of your curves are a landscape to behold.
Your heart's never-failing beat is attuned to our great Mother.

Nature is within every facet of you.
You are of the Earth.
She is of you.
You are one.

I FEEL AN OLD, NEW WAY EMERGING

I feel an old, new way emerging, a way that is what my heart wants, that feels good in my body, that honours all of me. A way that honours my rhythms, cycles and seasons; play and pleasure; action and rest; sensitivity and creativity; shadows and the void.

I feel its whispers beckoning me forth, letting me know that it's time to return to nature. To listen to her messages. Learn from her wisdom. Connect to her truth.

It tells me that I am here to co-create and be a conduit for love, compassion, peace and harmony.

By holding my own and staying true to my path, I will create what I came here to.

A way that supports others. That's in reverence for this planet. That considers the whole.

Do you feel it too?

THE SEASONS OF CREATION

Creation is a birthing process that we are constantly doing just by being alive.

We create our lives moment by moment.
We can create experiences we want to have.
We can create feelings we desire to embody.
We can create businesses, homes, friendships, art, and anything else we desire to.
We can create things yet unseen, as ideas come to us to be realised in the physical.
And of course, we can create life.

Creation is something we can play an active part in, and is cyclical, not linear. As I see it, it mirrors nature and the four main seasons in a year – spring, summer, autumn/fall and winter, through which Mother Earth creates.

These seasons can also be seen in the lunar cycle, with the new (or dark) moon representing winter, the waxing moon representing spring, the full moon as summer, and the waning moon representing autumn/fall.

The seasons can be found in the wisdom of the menstrual cycle, which in itself is a process of creation. These timings aren't fixed as everyone will experience them uniquely, but they roughly adhere to winter usually being the pre-menstruum and menstruating part of the cycle, spring is at the beginning of a new menstrual cycle as you emerge from menstruation, ovulation is the summer point, followed by autumn/fall as the cycle starts to move back again to menstruation. As an aside, for some people – they experience the qualities of each season differently. They feel more energised and alive in winter and needing to retreat in summer. So, if you are using the seasons of menstruation to guide you, always trust what you feel in each season. Your body knows better than anyone else can tell you.

Here are some of the qualities that each season embodies and the part they might play in creation. They are not prescriptive, they come from my (and others) observations of the seasons, and you may personally find the qualities for one resonate in another.

Spring

This is the season for visioning, planting seeds and intentions for what you want to create, alongside the guidance and energies that might be beckoning. It's also the season for beginning to nurture and nourish the seeds and vision, tending to them and starting to take grounded action.

Summer

This is the time for aligning with your desires and bringing your creations into the physical through inspired action. It is also often when you start to experience the pleasure of your desires becoming physical.

Autumn/fall

This is the releasing/letting go of any limitations, fears, resistance, blocks that are rising or perhaps being physically experienced, saying that you can't have or aren't aligned with the thing wanting to be created. It can be letting go of patterns, habits and/or behaviours that aren't serving you. It's healing and holding these parts so that they no longer create a vibrational misalignment within, with what is calling to be birthed.
This season can also hold the destruction of the old.

It's also about harvesting, calling on the parts of you that you may have been avoiding, out of fear or any other reason. It can be the literal harvesting of your creation. It could also be about beginning to embody or step into new parts which you may not have connected with and starting to claim them as who you are now.

Winter

This is the void, the holding, the space in between, to allow for growth or perhaps self-care, deep nourishment and healing – to be the vessel for all you will bring in. Often it seems like not much is happening at this time, but beneath the surface, so much is.

The process through which creations are birthed seems to tap into each of the different seasons, in varying degrees and ways. Sometimes a creation might call upon one season for the majority of the process and only draw upon a sprinkling of the others. Another creation might require equal amounts from each season. It totally depends on what the creation is, the person through which it's being birthed and the uniqueness of that journey.

For example, the process of making a baby starts in the spring with the seed fertilising the egg (plus, I feel there's a bit of summer in here as an orgasm occurs if the baby is being created through intercourse). But even before that there might be a need to tune into autumn/fall and let go of beliefs around having a baby, or perhaps even physical conditions that are coming up preventing this from happening. It then follows with a period of winter and gestation, and the mother being called to nourish deeply so that the unborn child can grow. This then ends with the summer and the baby coming into the physical through the process of aligned action and the body naturally doing this.

Another example is creating something in your life that you are being called to bring through, which is what this book will be tuning into, and as you will see, this might include different parts from different seasons.

To share briefly, bringing this book, *Embodied Creation*, into the physical followed this process (I go into more detail about this co-creation in the next part):

Spring – The idea started coming to me and I began to feel the whispers of it calling. I committed to writing it and signed a contract. More ideas came around what it was to include, and I began to follow that guidance, contacting the people globally from different backgrounds and ethnicities so that I could share their experiences in creation, with my guidance, showing that we are all more alike than different and that the process of creation doesn't discriminate.

Winter – I then went into a period of rest, having to stop the process and take time out for my own self-care and nourishment. It actually aligned with where I was at seasonally in the world, so came as no surprise that I felt more inward and needed to slow down. I put the book on hold as I surrendered to this process. Fully trusting and allowing as I knew this is what I was being called to do.

Autumn/fall – What followed next was a deep dive into my own inner blocks, stories, patterns and triggers rising, to let them go, to release them from my energy field and timeline, so that they no longer were playing out subconsciously, stopping me or holding me back in any way.

Spring – After going through the intensity of the inner work, the book came back to me with a renewed energy and readiness to be written. I started visioning how it would come together and include the different parts of my experience as well as the people I had been working with. I re-connected with everyone and began a refreshed process.

Summer – This is where I began to take massive action, connecting to the soul of the book (which I go more deeply into in the next part), and doing my part to co-create it and bring it into the physical.

Autumn/fall – Just as I thought I knew what this book was and had been bringing it together, it changed. It required me to let go of what I thought it was about and surrender. I had to grieve and take my ego out of the way, to let it become what it is now.

So, as you can see, this process is unique, it's messy and is not a linear process at all.

IT'S REALLY ABOUT CO-CREATION

When this book first started making itself known to me, I felt its energy beginning to whisper at me in early 2021, and it felt like it was going to be a book about manifesting. Creating what you desire in life and making that a reality – whatever that might be. It wanted me to have people from all over the world, from different walks of life, to show that manifesting is for everyone. This is how it began.

For those not so familiar with the process of connecting to the energy and soul of a book, it is an incredible support whereby you feel into (and you might see, hear, or just know it, as we all receive this information differently) the energy of the book as a life force which you can connect to, with its own characteristics, ways, guidance, etc. It is a wonderful process, which can reveal so much to co-create with you, and I will be sharing more on it later.

As my relationship and connection with the soul of this book, *Embodied Creation*, unfolded, it has taken me on quite a journey.

Grateful for the incredible community I've been gathering personally and through my business, I was able to connect with 11 people globally (including all continents except Antarctica) from different backgrounds who were all willing to be a part of this. All of them wanted to manifest something different including money, a new relationship, a home, a new business offering, a sanctuary, a fit and healthy body and even stepping into more visibility.

We began the process of creation together – digging into the stories and beliefs that were rising around why they couldn't have what they desired. Starting to connect to and vision this new reality they were each calling in.

Then it all stopped.

The energy disappeared.

There was absolutely nothing coming.

I actually began to feel quite tired when I connected to the energy of the book, and even the thought of continuing the work with the incredible people I had been connecting with was an absolute no-go.

So, I left it for a while. For a few months, I had to just let it be. I even wondered at one point if there was going to be a book, but from following the guidance for a few years now, I knew it was definitely a part of the process and I waited to see what would come next.

Eventually I was led to dive even deeper into my own healing journey, clearing and healing even more of my own stuff so that I can embody what I want to share and create on a whole new level. I was living with my parents back at my family home in Kenya where I grew up, and this is where many of my own beliefs, blocks and limitations around my own worth and confidence began (at least in this lifetime). So, this provided the perfect container to go deeper than I had ever before as being in this environment was bringing up all the memories and triggers that I thought I'd let go but hadn't.

I was being called to get support this time, to help hold and guide me through, and it came from my dear friend and Colour Mirrors mentor. Colour Mirrors is a system that leans into the power of colour as a mirror for what is going on inside, by using coloured bottles of oils and essences. The colours (and combinations) that you are drawn to and repelled by can reveal where there might be healing needed, as well as show your talents, gifts and more.

We went all in with deep, intense sessions every week and in between I would be doing a lot of my own inner work, processing, and releasing – using Colour Mirrors bottles (which are an incredibly powerful way to help your body heal and release on a cellular level). I can't even begin to tell you what an intense few weeks I had. We went into, held and healed countless stories and patterns from this lifetime and others, many tied into my own core wounds of feeling un-wanted, abandoned and unlovable (something I have been playing out since my adoption at birth) and giving away my power. I go into some of these in my book Embodied Business, as I take you through the chakras and blocks that can come up on the entrepreneurial journey, but this time I went deeper. Much deeper. I was being called to take this book further than I had first envisaged, and my own journey and inner work were integral to being able to hold what wanted to come through and to truly embodying it with integrity.

Almost as soon as I felt the intense inner work I was doing coming to a natural close, I began to feel the essence of *Embodied Creation* coming back to me. This time it felt different.

As this energy revealed itself, things changed. I had changed.

It felt deep.
It felt fierce.
It felt immense.
It was a definite She.

From this new place, She just had to meet Nicola, my incredible Unbound Press publisher, before She took me further on our journey together, which I share about in the next part. She just had to be held by another gorgeous soul-friend and channel as She knew through this space and her energy another aspect of it could be held and brought to light.

The way I was working with others around the globe changed: it became about talking to them and supporting them with a small part of the creation process in a conscious way, rather than all of it, as we are creating in every moment. Allowing for conversations around this, asking what their hearts wanted to create, learning from each one, and affirming that we are all more alike than different, and work needs to be done collectively on a global scale from a root level to truly begin to make changes.

She revealed parts as I was ready to hold them. At times I had to ask her to slow down, to help me as I felt overwhelmed by all the information that seemingly didn't connect (my mind likes order and to see the bigger picture).

This book has been a deep and layered co-creation between myself, her fierce and feminine energy, my publisher, the sensitive souls and clients I have had the privilege of working with and speaking to, as well as other healers, guides and space holders who have held me throughout the process.

THE ESSENCE OF EMBODIED CREATION

Whilst connecting to the soul of this book after I had done more of my own inner work, I got to a place where She felt ready to share with me again. Her powerful energy took over and I was taken on a journey beneath the ground. Down, down, down, we went to a cave buried way beneath the surface. I was left there at the entrance, not able to go any further. It took a few days waiting there, feeling an energy behind the rocks, feeling that there was something coming, but I couldn't go any further.

I just had to show up daily in my visualisations and be present. Still. Patient. Waiting. I later realised that the energy was getting to know me. Feeling my commitment to being with it, and whether I was ready to hold it. It needed to feel that it was in safe hands, and that I was willing to let it emerge and be exactly what it is.

We deepened our connection whilst I sat at that cave entrance every day for a few days. Eventually it began to open and it took me through the cave, and we went even deeper, into the depths of the Earth. We went down into the underworld, passing through darkness, murkiness, orange haze, lots and lots of orange. But it kept leading me onwards, travelling together for a while.

Finally, we got to a point where we could go no further. Then the winds came. The ground rumbled. The fires came. The tides washed in. The elements made themselves known.

They released, they cleared. They made space.

When they were finished, I was taken to a beautiful cove. It felt like the tropics and there was the smell of salt in the air.

As I waited, staring out onto the cove, I began to see what seemed like hundreds of beings rising from the waters and the surrounding shadows. Beings from different cultures, places and lineages, creatures, insects, fairies, dragons, elves, mer-people, the physical embodiment of so many different types of energies from all times, all places, all walks of life. Some were human, others hybrid human, most were not human at all. They began to slowly lift their heads, gently coming up, beginning to look in my direction.

I felt that these were the ones that had been shut out and locked away, chased, banished, for carrying and sharing truths, for being ugly, being unacceptable, for caring, for healing and helping, for speaking up, for not conforming. These were the ones that had been silenced.

I can still vividly see and feel all their different parts – they each carry different qualities and strengths that make up the whole: courage, holding, empathy, compassion, love, generosity, peace, beauty, also a deep and powerful fierceness. Together it felt like the embodied energy of the Divine feminine.

As their heads rose, they began to show me the space around their throats and how it connects to the heart. It's as though their skins had been shielding this space. Holding it in safety and protection. As they lifted their heads up, their throats began to open; they were showing me the strength and power held here. A power that it is now time to remember, reveal and actively tune into.

One of the beings in human form then came to me; she felt like an elder, a wise woman, one who had seen it all. I intuitively felt her name to be Rayya. Without words, she shared that the truth is carried in all the waters that come from the Earth. It's also carried in the womb and has been passed down within each and every one of us through the waters we are held in before being born. We carry this truth in our cells, in our veins.

Many of us are feeling it stirring, as the time is now for it to come back and be shared, so that globally we can use it to create change. It needs us all over the world to know it, to be a voice for it, to share it, and support others with it.

It's the current and power of creation, the essence of all that is.
It's the energy of beginnings and endings.
It is life, death and rebirth.

It has the power to build and destroy and rebuild.
It is the power to be and do anything.
It can change lives, it can change the world.

Those of us here to hold and spread this wisdom have gone, or are going, through initiations of our own. As it needs us to hold space for it to breathe, to release, to shed, to grieve all that it has endured from being buried, abused and controlled. It is through our waters – our tears, our sweat, our blood, as well as our screams, our words, our bodies – that we have been, and are still, releasing.

Rayya then took my hand and pointed to one side of the cove, up towards the mountains, where I could see a towering, magnificent pine forest. Without speaking, she shared that this is where we must go. This is where the key lies.

We travelled upwards towards the trees, and in a moment I could feel myself amidst their glorious strength. We then went down the side of one, following its roots, further down again, we were falling. We landed in a cave-like space, with a soft glowing green-yellow merkaba shaped crystal. She invited me to place my hands on it within hers to feel its messages.

As I did, I felt my heart begin to glow within the space, emitting the same light as this crystal.

As my heart connected with this crystal heart, it felt as though it was tuning back into the heart of Gaia and together they shone the brightest light throughout the cave, and I felt the deepest sense of magic and possibility. All the darkness had disappeared, and I felt so much tenderness, abundance, gentleness, kindness, expansion, freedom, love. I felt anything and everything I have ever wanted is possible, and the heart holds the key.

THE HEART HOLDS THE KEY

After seeing, feeling and deeply experiencing the wisdom and strength of the heart in the cave I was taken to, I fully get the power of this centre within each of us.

Interestingly, before I fully settled in to write this book, my word for the year was 'heart'. I came to it from a place of loss, grief and letting go of a relationship, realising that I hadn't been tending to my heart at all, and intuitively knew and felt that I needed to hold space for it. So, I began a daily heart connection practice, where I held my heart and tuned into its energy and anything it would like to share with me.

In the beginning, my heart felt tender, delicate and vulnerable. It was often a soft pink or coral colour and needed lots of protection around it. I just needed to hold it and be present with it, so that's what I did. Every time I did this, even if it only took a couple of minutes, I would feel the shift in my energy – becoming more grounded, connected and embodied.

As the process went on, my heart started showing me different energies and colours. I felt it as a spring green energy, dancing and beginning to feel more curious. I felt it as vast as the cosmos, a silvery indigo portal taking me into other dimensions. Some days it felt soft, delicately unfurling, its exquisite fragility deeply present. At other times it was a deep red of life force that felt grounding and a firm reminder of my physicality. It truly was (and continues to be) a magical experience, which I highly recommend devoting yourself to.

Going back to the cave. The light of my heart shone out into the space, illuminating the darkness and revealing to me what I truly desired.

The heart is the key to unlocking the truth.
It holds ancient wisdom inside.
It holds the power of manifestation, creation, of bringing desires

into the physical.
Of connection, empathy, support and love for one another.
Of a collaborative, inclusive, unified way of living.
It recognises the oneness and how we are all a mirror of one another.
It reminds us that we are the same.
It brings us home to ourselves.
It has the wisdom to bring this into existence.

This truth is buried deep inside many at the moment.
We have to spend time with it.
We have to tend to it.
Be with it.
Let it begin to surface.
This is where the key is.

The guidance, knowing, support and wisdom to bring this world into the physical comes from the heart.

The higher heart chakra is connected and a part of this. This is the space between the heart and throat, above the thymus gland, which is where the heart and throat wisdom merges. It brings together the manifesting power of the voice, speaking it into existence, with the truth and wisdom of the heart, where we can truly create from a place of oneness.

TENDING TO YOUR HEART

This is the way that creation will happen that considers the whole, that considers 'we' as well as 'me'. This is where you will truly connect with what is wanting to come through you. This is where we, as a collective, need to tune in regularly, so that we feel our hearts open and connect to something greater. Tending to your heart is a portal into the truth of who you are, who we are, how we can help to bring the world back into balance and create offerings, communities, opportunities, and ways that genuinely care for one another and this planet.

I like to see all of the hearts of humanity connected, as well as connected into the heart of Mother Earth and the Divine. It's just that so many of us have blocked or almost severed this connection, it might take some 'heart-holding' to re-connect fully. As a sensitive soul, this may not be the case for you, but you may feel that it's not safe to trust your heart. Perhaps you don't let it open fully as feeling so much can be overwhelming. Maybe it's something else.

When we tend to our own hearts, we connect to our feelings – which are absolutely key for creating – as they enable us to firstly connect to a true desire, and then as you connect to the feeling/s of that desire, made possible in the heart, you also bring it closer to the physical. We also feel held and at home so we naturally want to give more and tune into a bigger purpose and meaning.

Here are some very simple practices that I have used to help me connect to my own heart and tend to its needs, as well as learn to trust it.

A daily heart connection

As mentioned, I have a daily heart practice of placing one hand on my heart to see and feel its energy. Bring your attention to your heart space – noticing any colours, shapes, feelings and anything else. Then simply stay present with it, acknowledging and observing it, exactly as it is.

Ask your heart what it needs

Following the steps from above, simply tune into your heart and ask it what it needs today. Then if you are able to, give to it what it needs. This might involve practically doing something for your heart and self, or it might involve visualising or imagining yourself giving it to it.

Sometimes it might be hard to connect with your heart, especially if it has been a while or we're not sure what to trust. This is where oracle cards or tarot cards might come in handy. Shuffle the deck and allow one to pop up, or choose one, whilst asking the question, 'What does my heart need today?'

Connect your heart to the heart of Mother Earth

Lie on the ground, outside if possible (but not essential), and feel your heart beating in your chest. See if you can draw your energy down, to the centre of the Earth. Feel the heartbeat of the great Mother. Simply breathe into this, even just the idea of it, and let your heartbeat align with that of Mother Earth.

Hold your heart

I do this now without even thinking, and it's so simple but so powerful. Just holding your heart for a second or two throughout your day asks you to slow down and re-connect to this part of your body. Bringing your attention down from your mind into the portal of the heart space, back in your body.

Create a heart list

What are the things that make your heart happy? What are the things that light up your heart? Perhaps it's an intimate moment, watching a beautiful sunset, feeling the magnificence of a forest or the ocean, staring at the stars, cooking a beautiful meal, connecting with your loved ones. I invite you to write a list of 30 things that feel good to YOUR heart and then do one a day, every day.

Opening your heart

Yoga is a wonderful practice to support you here as there are many postures that guide you to gently open the space around your heart. You can also support your heart to open by doing something kind for someone else, showing compassion or kindness to another soul, perhaps being vulnerable with someone or connecting with how you really feel.

There is a guided visualisation to take you a little deeper into your heart and support you in the resources section.

CONNECTING WITH YOUR GUIDANCE

Deepening your relationship with your intuition and guidance will support you to trust more in yourself and what you are co-creating. Find the answers within, feel the energy of what wants to come through you and create a life that's aligned with the rhythms of the natural world as it tunes into the wisdom available to all of us. Above all, we need to slow down, stop even, and listen deeply as this is where we will hear/know/feel/see/receive the guidance.

Here are some ways I have fine-tuned connecting with my intuition to support myself.

Create space

My intuition speaks to me when I am not rushing and working from a busy head. When I am in a space of fun, pleasure and just being, it speaks to me more loudly. Often when I ask for guidance on a particular thing I won't get an answer straight away; it will come suddenly when I least expect it, or I'll just *know* how to move forward. It's very subtle and doesn't always come clearly. Be patient, and listen closely.

Eat clean

My intuition is often loudest when I am cleansing or eating only fresh food! As I clear out the foods and drinks that can cause my energy to be pulled in different directions, I am brought even deeper into myself, and I am so much more connected. Yet another reminder of the power of being in the body!

Tune in to my cycle

I've now learned I'm most connected with my intuition in the autumn and winter parts of my cycle, the yin phases. During this period I often spend more time doing morning pages and journaling, as this is another way I can connect deeply with my intuition, asking whatever I need.

Listen and trust

I always listen to my intuition when it guides me. This has meant at times not taking action and not forcing things. Instead, I trust that I am supported and know that when the time is right, I will be given the guidance to move forward. For a recovering impatient person, this is not always easy, but it is essential.

Something interesting also happened with my intuition and the way it connected with me during my journey with Covid. Firstly, it disappeared totally when I had Covid. I couldn't hear, feel, or 'know' anything like I used to. I felt quite naked without it, having generally had a previously loud intuition that spoke to me. Some fear arose and I found myself wondering if it would come back. What happened was it returned a few weeks later in a much more embodied way. It was this deep inner feeling and knowing that was, and still is, so present throughout my day. I don't have to ask it things like it's a separate part of me. I just know now. As so many of us have experienced Covid and the world is changing so fast, I invite you to feel into whether your intuition is changing or has changed at all. It may change again too – just remember the importance of connecting with it, letting it be what it wants to be, and deeply honouring this part of ourselves.

TRUST YOURSELF

At the end of the day, only you know your path.
Only you know your truth.
You are the one living in your body, with your experiences, stories, relationships, feelings and life.

You have to learn to listen and trust the wisdom you hold inside.

There will be signs: something you hear on the radio; a headline you see; a creature that appears to symbolise something; nature will commune with you; there will be guidance from others – intuitives, children, pets and more, and this can all absolutely support you on your journey.

But if it doesn't feel good to you, it's not right for you.
If it feels off, it's not right for you.

Your guidance is wise and can show you ways that you might not think of and that others can't tell you. It may come as a feeling, a knowing, a hunch, an idea, a moment of synchronicity. It will support you to go on the journey that you are being called to in this lifetime.

It needs to be trusted, you need to build a relationship with it, surrender to it and let it lead and honour its wisdom.

WHAT KIND OF WORLD DO YOU WANT TO LIVE IN?

As a sensitive soul, you have a gift, an innate quality that means you can see, feel, touch, hear, know, and intuit so much.

You know where change is needed.
You want fairness and equality.
You want harmony and beauty.
Peace and balance.

You are here to create it.
You are here to embody it.

First start by deeply tuning in and asking, *What kind of world do I want to live in*?

What does it feel like?
What does it look like?
What does it mean?
What does it encompass?

Keep holding this vision.
Treasure it, protect it, keep it close by.
For you'll need to come back to it.
Some may call it your 'why'.

EMBODIED CREATION PRACTICE

I invite you to deeply feel into the kind of world you want to live in. Describe it in as much detail as you can. As you do this, allow yourself to begin to feel what this brings up in you. What emotions are rising? Really begin to feel them in your body. Letting them get stronger and more vivid as you connect with them.

Do this as often as you can as it will really help to anchor in this vision, which in turn will lead you to start to be, do and eventually have experiences which mirror these emotions and will start to lay the foundations for creating this reality.

'BE A CHANGE-MAKER' PROMPTS

Here are a few prompts to feel into the areas that you can bring your energy and creative efforts to, in whatever way you are being called.

- What gets your blood boiling?
- What are you passionate about?
- What makes you want to speak up?
- What moves your heart?
- What brings you to tears?
- What do you wish was different in the world?
- What do you wish more people knew?
- What does true wealth mean to you?
- What does abundance for all look like to you?
- If anything was possible, what would you do?

WHAT IF?

What if we were so in touch with our bodies, all their signs and messages, that we cared for and tended to them like a newborn child?

What if every time we felt pain, sadness, fear or anything else that didn't feel good, we held these emotions and feelings, listened to them, let them speak to us, tell us what they need? Then we sat with them, held them and gave them all we could to support them.

What if we fed our bodies with only water and fresh, sun- and Earth-nourished foods that give us nutrients, energy, all the sustenance we need to feel deeply alive?

What if we felt so deeply connected to Earth as our home that we cared how we are treating it and restored the balance of giving and receiving?

What if we stopped for a moment to listen to others? Stopped needing to be right, have the last word, and truly considered where they might be coming from so we extended more compassion and empathy.

What if we became so comfortable with ourselves, we could feel content simply be-ing, even in times that felt empty, void-like?

What if we stopped filling spaces with stuff, food, noise, everything and anything, and instead we spent time listening, feeling, and hearing our own inner guidance?

What would this world be like?

YOUR FEELINGS ARE THE FORCE THAT DRIVES CREATION

We create the world we want to live in through our desires and the way we want to feel. So many of us don't actually know what it means to feel good. To feel real joy. To feel deep love – for ourselves and others.

Much of the world looks to consumerism, addictions or other fast fixes to feel good, and yes, of course, we have needs and can want things, but what is the feeling behind it all? What are we trying to fill? To satiate?

Lasting, true joy and feeling good comes from deep within. In my experience, it comes from doing the inner healing, releasing and learning to be fully with yourself. From returning to nature's embrace and remembering we are here for a short time.

From this space, you want to create for the good of all.
You know we are not separate, not in competition, not alone.
You desire to live a life that feels good from inside, not the other way around.

EMBODIED CREATION PROMPTS

Think about what you crave on a daily, weekly or even monthly basis. Is it certain foods like chocolate or something crunchy? Do you fill all of your time with meaningless TV, shopping or something else? Think about what you are looking for underneath it all, and then ask yourself, how can I begin to give this to myself and/or create this feeling in my life?

For example, with chocolate, maybe you are craving comfort and love, and so I invite you to come up with a number of ways to start showing love and care to yourself, such as cooking a healthy meal, going for a walk, taking a bath. If you fill all your time, perhaps you are feeling lonely and are looking for connection and intimacy. So, how could you begin to connect with yourself and really be with yourself, or even others?

This may bring up more things such as questioning one's own worth, deservedness and/or more, and so I invite you to dig deeper if that's what you are being called to do, but also reach out for support if you need it. We have a lot of un-binding to do from all of our childhoods and beliefs. I share more about this in the 'Creation blocks' section.

THE CREATION PROCESS

This section gives an overview of the process of co-creation –
what it is and how you can co-create with Gaia. It dives into the
feminine and masculine energies, their qualities and the part they
play in creation. It looks at the role of Mothers here too. Then
there is a sub-section on 'Getting started' which you can use to
support you to begin.

THE FEMININE PATH OF CREATION

The spark will come to you.
A wink of inspiration.
You'll feel it in your bones.
Know in your waters that you are here to co-create it.
You'll commit and begin.
Thinking that you've got this.

But, as you get going.
She likely won't give you much.
It will come in pieces.
You will be given the next step.
It may not make sense.
You won't know how it fits together.
What it's going to look like.
Even up to the end.
It will feel messy, all over the place.
The farthest thing from linear.
You may want to give up.
Think WTF, this isn't working.

But have faith. Trust. Like never before.
You'll feel her holding you.
Know she has got you.
Her unwavering support is always there.
With her fierce, mothering strength.
She won't let you down.
She will put her arm around you.
Show you the way.
Piece by piece.
Step by step.

Right until the 'end'.
When you can look back at the journey.
With its ebbs, flows, ups and downs.
The spiral that led you.
Up to that magnificent moment.

IT'S TIME FOR BIRTHING THE NEW

The world needs you to birth its new energies.
Through books, businesses, projects, ideas, and other creations.

Doing your inner work to align, hold and support yourself.
To bring forth creations without trauma and baggage.

Tuning into your power as a creator.
Embodying your wisdom and love.

To birth from a place of non-attachment.
To birth from the heart, not the ego.

To birth for the act of simply creating beauty.
With intentions of oneness, compassion, collaboration,
togetherness and empathy.

It needs you to hold it in a womb-like cocoon.
Being the one to bring it into the physical.
This is how the world births the new.
It needs you to allow it to come through.

CO-CREATING WITH THE NON-PHYSICAL

Learning to co-create with energies beyond the physical is something that continues to add to the enchantment of my life in so many ways. It also feels like I am bringing something through beyond my small, or ego, self. It challenges and stretches me (in a good way) and deeply supports me to become more and more ME, as the creations that come through each have their own needs, way and guidance, which call me to go deep, heal and grow to align with them.

I first learned about connecting to the essence or life force of something non-physical in a women's circle I was a part of, as I was guided to connect to the energy of the name of the circle, to feel its essence, its qualities, and anything else that came up for me, to co-create the space we were holding together. I was quite blown away and found it to be an extremely powerful experience as I could feel and see the energy so strongly. It had a distinctly unique personality, was totally grounded and had so many magical colours and energies combined (representative of all of us in the circle).

It was quite a magical moment for me as I felt this deep support available, and really felt the potential of creating in this way if I applied it to other areas, as it took it beyond just me, so I felt like I didn't have to do it all alone. There was guidance there if I chose to connect to it. It also re-connected me to the magic I always felt as a child, just *knowing* my teddy bears were alive and feeling all the energies of the unseen (fairies, tree spirits and dragons) in the garden.

Since then, I have connected to the energy and qualities of my business (and every offering within it), letting it guide me. I also learned to connect to the energy of each of my books with the wonderful guidance of my publisher, Nicola. Today I support empath entrepreneurs to connect to and co-create with the energies of their businesses and offers, as an integral part of their work.

Here are a few things I have learned from co-creating with what is calling to come through. More often than not, you are taken on a journey beyond what you could imagine with your rational mind. Often the process is much slower than you might want it to be, as in our western society we tend to want everything yesterday. (There can absolutely be exceptions here, for example my book *Embodied Business* came through fully in less than three weeks.) You will usually be guided to tend to yourself as the vessel for what you are bringing through. Sometimes you might have to let go completely and totally rearrange things before it comes into the physical. You will likely need to relinquish any thoughts of control and trying to see an end result, as it often won't make itself known until the very end.

All I can say for sure is you have to deepen your connection with what is coming through, and like any relationship, it needs to be nurtured. The 'Seasons of creation' will support you here.

EMBODIED CREATION PRACTICE

You are probably wondering how to do this. There isn't one set way. You could simply write down the question, 'What is calling to come through me?' and then start writing in your non-dominant hand, allowing what comes up. You could do a practice like Morning Pages and again ask the same question, seeing what comes up over time. You can also just let the inspiration come to you or become aware of signs and messages. I share more on this in the next part, 'Co-creating with Gaia'. There is also a guided visualisation on how to do this in general and in the 'Co-create with the soul of your business' resources at the end.

As an aside, I have always found it easy to visualise and get strong images and feelings when I connect to energies. However, you might find it easier to feel the energy, simply know it, or you might hear it or experience it in another way – however it comes to you is perfect.

Lastly, however you are being called to create, we don't always know what our contribution will be. It may be something activating and visionary that provokes and incites. It may be a soothing balm or something of beauty that comforts and/or delights. Every creation is valuable and needed. Don't get caught up in the outcome, container, vessel or form that it will take. Let go of what you think it needs to look like.

CO-CREATING WITH GAIA

To deeply lean into the wisdom of Mother Earth and begin to bring through the creations she is calling to be birthed at this time, you need to deeply commit to connecting with her in a multitude of ways. As many ways as you can think of. Here are a few to get you started.

- Do some gardening.
- Nurture a pot plant.
- Lie on the ground (outside if possible).
- Take a walk in nature.
- Place your hands on a tree.
- Look up at the sky.
- Listen to the birds.
- Make creations from fallen twigs, leaves, etc.
- Go wild swimming.
- Walk barefoot.
- Eat foods straight from nature.

As you do this, you will begin to hear, feel, and know her guidance and what she is calling to create through you.

Whilst writing this book, I was blessed to be in Kenya, where I grew up, which also happens to be the birthplace of creation and a land of vast beauty and nature. Since being in Kenya, I have created my own daily communion practice with nature, which has mainly involved walking in a lush forest with a river flowing through or sitting/lying in the garden and just being.

As this became my way of life, I started to notice nature much more. I started to appreciate what I normally would have taken for granted. The orange caterpillars that emerge from the wood beams and almost as quickly create cocoons, before becoming moths seemingly overnight. The colobus monkeys with their wise, old faces that sweep through the trees with elegance and grace. The dancing butterflies, which dazzle me daily with their turquoise, orange, white, yellow and blue hues. Even the green snake that came to say hello at my window.

I wistfully admire the bougainvillea, that seems to thrive the hotter it gets, as it reminds me of my school days. I adore the lilac Jacaranda flowers that blossom only at certain times of the year. I notice the hibiscus flowers, which seem to pop with sensuality before the monkeys get to them.

I have felt the fire of the sunshine warming me to my bones. I have earthed myself, lying with my heart connected to hers. I have felt the power of the wind filling my lungs just before a storm. The rains never fail to take my breath away as they beat down with a ferocity that I've only ever seen in the tropics, before parting into glorious sunshine.

Nature became my muse once again, after being so closely connected with it in school and it inspiring all of my creations.

I created chakras dragon energy paintings as I connected with the trees outside my window, feeling their life force calling to come through. I sketched leaves and bark patterns that caught my attention, finding comfort in their geometry and form. It re-connected me with my heart, opening it after decades of feeling I had to guard it from harsh London-City-living. It fuelled my soul, my passion, and my creative life force.

Nature became the inspiration and golden thread weaving through this book, as I was reminded that creation is nature, nature is creation.

When you connect with her closely, you can't help but feel her energy, itching to be expressed.

As I see it, we are once again being asked to come back to nature, to create with her.

EMBODIED CREATION PRACTICE
I invite you to connect with nature in whatever way you are being called, with the intention of asking what you are being called to create at this time.

There's an additional visualisation at the end to feel into the energy of Gaia and receive any guidance on what you are being called to co-create.

Get out of your own way

As I have shared, for the majority of the time I spent with *Embodied Creation* and her energy, I thought it was going to be a book about manifesting and creating what we think we want. More money, a home, love, businesses, clients, etc. I knew co-creating fit in there, but it hadn't felt like the main theme.

What emerged and only made itself fully clear in the last few weeks of writing (!) was that it's about creating what wants to come through you for the good of all, not so much what we think we want.

I had to get out of the way, letting go of any pre-conceptions I had that I was ever in control, and let the whole process unfold and guide me.

It's quite a metaphor for 'Creation' as a whole, and it does make me smile, as She always knew more than I could wrap my logical mind around. It's just such a confirmation of following through, letting it come, letting it guide you, staying the course, trusting – damn-bloody-trusting – right to the end.

Embodied Creation prompt

I invite you to let go of what you think you want to create, to allow the space for what wants to come. Let the creation come through you. Let it be what it wants to be.

Ask yourself, 'Is what I desire to create from ego or soul and heart?' Be honest with yourself.

Embodied Creation share

Marta was connecting to the soul of her business and received the guidance that she is not supposed to have a business anymore; instead, she is here to share energy, meditations and healing, but not through the vessel of a business. This was a big realisation for her, having had a business for years and trying to find a way through with it. A lot was rising around whether she should have one, how she felt, what her identity would be without it.

67

After some time sitting with this guidance, I asked her what she was being called to create and this is what came. 'I'm being called to re-create myself. Everything has fallen away over the past few months, and I feel now like I'm picking up the pieces. I want to be the best version of myself which will hopefully enrich everything else.'

Sometimes the guidance we receive might throw us, pull the rug out from underneath us, and make us question who and what we are. It might be to let everything go. It's an invitation to trust, allow what wants to come and know you are here to create the new. It might look and feel different to what we know already. Also, know that it might not be forever. Things sometimes need to change for a while and then they come back in a different way that's more aligned for you.

FEMININE AND MASCULINE ENERGIES IN CREATION

Feminine and masculine energy is integral to creation as they both play their part as different, complementary and opposite forces of energy. These energies go beyond one's personality and physical anatomy, and we all carry both of these energies to varying degrees.

Sometimes we can tune into and embody both ourselves, for example, when we are bringing a creative idea into the world such as a book, an offering, or something else. Sometimes we need another to provide some of one or both of the energies for us, for example, in the creation of a human baby, or perhaps for bigger ideas and projects which might need a lot of energy and support. It's ideal to have different people with their various strengths and balance of different energies all contributing, adding to the whole.

Here is an overview of these energies in creation, what their strengths are, as well as what can happen if one of these is used out of harmony with the other.

Feminine

In creation, the feminine is the mysterious, intuitive, sensitive, visioning part. It can connect with the magical and unseen, deeply feeling what needs to come in. It asks for a level of trust as it is based on the energetics, rather than physical action, and so is less tangible.

It then tends to nurture what is being created, allowing the journey and unfolding of it. It leans into pleasure, enjoyment, play and deep levels of self-nourishment as essential to the journey of creation; it knows that from this place, inspiration often comes. It is kind, tender, and compassionate, creating to benefit the whole.

It knows when to stop and be, embodying the power of stillness and the void, allowing the flow, trusting the inner guidance will come, and not needing to get every detail. It honours the Divine timing of life.

The out-of-balance feminine in creation can fall into patterns of victimhood, manipulation, co-dependency, neediness and giving away personal power. It lacks faith and trust and is disconnected from receiving any guidance, including inner wisdom. Often, a lot of emphasis is placed on approval from others, which leads to insecurities, doubts, fears, anxiety and other issues.

Masculine

The masculine in creation is the more expansive and outward part that takes action. It can have a clear, focused direction and is the container that provides protection, stability, systems, structures and support for what is being created. Often, this is to hold the feminine, as the masculine respects the wisdom of this energy and works in partnership with it.

It can be courageous and disciplined, and it can persevere in dedication to a common desired outcome. It uses the ego as a driving force to benefit the whole.

The out-of-balance masculine in creation focuses heavily on the ego and wanting to gain for the self, rather than the whole. It can abuse power, be competitive and abusive, as well as controlling and aggressive. It overworks (with the output of energy far exceeding the input), depleting its resources and any natural feminine energy present. This leads to burnout, anxiety, depression, insomnia and other health issues. It is disconnected from any sense of trust in oneself or another power.

The current dominating way of creating in most of the world, but particularly in the west, is through the masculine, and many believe it to be the only way to create, through pushing to make something happen, having to constantly be taking action, more often than not at the expense of others and one's own health and happiness.

The feminine way takes a lot more faith and trust as we are asked to let go of what we know and lean into something we can't physically see and can only feel or intuit. This is hard for many as we are so disconnected from our own feelings, and also feel so separate from any other form of support, thinking that the only way is to do it for ourselves, which lends itself to the masculine way.

I believe we need to find our own harmony between these energies, leaning into and finding a way forward that taps into the strengths of each, but it starts with deep kindness, compassion and gentleness for ourselves exactly as we are. We need to re-connect to our bodies, their feelings, their wisdom, and learn to trust ourselves. As we do this, we remember our connection to more than ourselves, to one another, to Earth, to a higher power (whatever we choose to believe that is), and we begin to tune into our innate power as creators.

I also deeply know and feel that we are more powerful at creating than we have ever believed ourselves to be, and the more we lean into the power of the feminine and her energies in nature, using the power of intention, holding the vision, deeply knowing and trusting, then the more effortless, magical and awe-inspiring our creating and creations will become. Whilst some tune into this and know this already, we still live in a society which has become more in favour of the masculine energies, and so some adjusting and harmonising is needed to even begin to honour the feminine energies.

THE POWER OF THE FEMININE WITH THE HOLDING OF THE MASCULINE

The feminine holds power in its ability to intuit, to vision, to bring about a desire into the physical through sheer inner-knowing and magnetism.

But, for centuries the feminine has been shut down, locked away, as the dark masculine became the dominating force. The dark masculine's ego couldn't accept and honour the feminine for the gift that it is and brings, so it had to control it.

Now the time has come to honour the strengths and qualities of both.

The feminine needs to let itself be held by the masculine, cherishing the masculine for the support it brings and the part it plays in creation. The feminine needs to learn to receive from the masculine and begin to trust it again.

The masculine has had a lot of bad rap in our patriarchal society, as it has become unbalanced and embodies many qualities at one end of the spectrum. However, the Divine masculine is needed more than ever, especially for the feminine to feel safe to come back, and also so it doesn't swing right back in the other direction of the out-of-balance matriarchal.

The Divine masculine is the holding part, the part that can feel like home. That honouring and safe space from which to let the feminine side flow, dance and live in her raw, cyclical wildness.

Unfortunately for so many of us, we don't know what that feels like. If anything, we've been shown the opposite, coming from families and homes which lacked holding and stability, instead feeling turbulent and un-grounded, even if the best intentions were present.

The masculine needs to recognise the value in the feminine – its innate wisdom, how it restores and brings a deeper connection with ourselves, each other, and Planet Earth.

As the masculine opens once again to the power of the feminine, it can begin to feel a safe space of holding for its fullness to come forward.

For in wholeness is the essence of creation needed on the planet at this time.

FEMININE POWER

There's a gentleness to feminine power. But don't mistake that for weakness. It's powerful as fuck!

It is the force of nature, from the delicate kiss of sunshine and spring greens, tender in their unfurling, to the bounty of nature bursting with abundance, colour and ripeness at the peak of summer. It moves into the chaos and swirling of autumn, letting all that must shed be gone. It's the stillness in the depths of winter where it retreats to replenish and restore, deeply nourishing before the time comes to peek its head up once more.

The time has come for feminine power to be restored.
For feminine power to come forward.
For feminine power to lead.

Feminine power cares about the planet, all humans, all creatures, all life. It is fierce, it's mothering, it's protective.

Feminine power supports others, and creates communities, collaborations, belonging. It is the force that knows we must do this together, that there is no other way.

Feminine power trusts itself deeply. It knows the wisdom we carry within and calls on it, never wavering in its faith of it, trusting the path it leads.

Feminine power is vulnerable, it lets itself be curious, it lets itself not know, it knows that from this place of truth there is empathy and wholeness.

The feminine has the power to change the world, creating for the good of the whole as it embodies these qualities:

Compassion

Compassion fuels empathy, kindness and love for one another. It reminds us that we are all in this together. What another experiences is a result of what we, collectively, have created. It might not be us directly, but it is as a result of the systems, society and, let's face it, a lot of the time, the patriarchy that we have been born into and may still feed knowingly or un-knowingly. With compassion, we can begin to take action to support others, because we get it. We can feel or at least empathise with what they feel. We create to empower, to revitalise and support the whole.

Nurture

I feel this to be the highest form of Divine feminine leadership, as it encourages and allows others to be exactly who they are. It leans into the wisdom of the heart, intuiting and encouraging with care, so that an individual's own unique essence and qualities are nurtured and brought forward.

Often when this happens, there's an allowing for what wants to come through that is unique to each individual. It holds space for them to birth in some way their creative expression, which is their unique magic that they are here to give to the world.

Community

Intrinsically linked to compassion and nurture, forming a community fosters a sense of belonging. Whether it's a number of communities which overlap, dance together and co-exist, this is a space to flourish and grow alongside others. A space where individual qualities can come together, to co-create, to go deeper, to be even more. This is where human connection is felt, growth is enriched, and we don't feel so alone.

PRACTICAL WAYS TO EMBODY THE FEMININE AND MASCULINE FOR CONSCIOUS CO-CREATION

Diving into the feminine

This is an invitation to let yourself dive deeply into the feminine. We have been operating from the masculine, or at least the majority have, for so long that we need to let the pendulum swing as far as it needs to in the other direction, to feel the opposite, so it re-calibrates and finds its natural landing space.

I share many ways you can do this in my book *Embodied*, but here are some specifically to open up and tune into your feminine centres for creation.

Explore and get to know your feminine side

Creativity: Take yourself on a journey with your creativity, and allow yourself to create in any way that appeals to you, just because, not for any outcome. Also, let yourself think outside of the box. Creativity doesn't have to mean painting or doing something typical; it could be playing with fallen leaves, making something from old bits lying around the house, moving your body into different shapes. Whatever you can think of.

Be-ing: Spend more time be-ing, in stillness, without an agenda – if you can, do this in nature, to connect with the natural rhythms of Mother Earth.

Pleasure: Explore pleasure and what that means to you. What brings you pleasure, what do you consider pleasure, how do you receive pleasure?

Trust: How can you trust more? Where don't you trust? Perhaps you can get to know and play with your intuition more. Maybe you can let someone else make all your decisions for a day. What would it take to trust yourself and the Divine more?

Lean into the deep wisdom of your body

Let the vessel of your body teach you and show you the way. I invite you to use the energy centres of the heart and sacral space (a few inches beneath your belly button) as your starting points, as these are considered the feminine chakras. Tune into these portals by perhaps visualising them, or holding them and connecting with them, and then ask for their guidance, holding space for any whispers and nudges that you might hear, feel, receive, or just know.

You can also connect to your hips – let them sway, move intuitively, feel their way around, leading the rest of your body if it is being called.

The left side of the body is considered the feminine side (and the right the masculine) as this is the part governed by the right brain hemisphere, which is the more creative, intuitive side, so you can also be mindful of what the left-hand side of your body is telling you.

In ancient Mystery school teachings that centred around womb awakening, the lower half of the body, from the belly button down, is considered the feminine part. So you could deeply connect with this part and spend time nurturing it and listening to its messages.

There is also a visualisation in the resources section called 'Connecting to feminine power' to begin to feel this energy as a current rising from Mother Earth if it calls you.

Embodying the Divine masculine that supports the feminine

As we each carry both energies within us, we need to let the masculine energy in us be the holding and space from which the powerful Divine feminine can feel supported. Alongside this can be receiving that holding and support from others who perhaps embody more masculine energy, or at least bring those qualities to the table.

Here are a couple of prompts for you to begin to feel into where you currently are at with this, as so many of us have come from a predominantly masculine energy as the foundation.

- *How do you feel about systems, structures and processes?*
  Notice what this brings up and how you feel in your body.
  Many people that I have worked with, spoken to, and interviewed who are more in tune with their feminine side have an aversion to these things. Systems and processes represent the rigidity, the boring, the controlling aspects that the feminine doesn't want to bow to. I find if this is the case, people might even run from them, and as such find that their feminine is often quite un-grounded, floaty and doesn't feel safe to land. If this is you, what would it take to get curious about how these might support you, how can you begin to see them as essential to grounding your feminine at this time?
  On the flip side, if you feel excited by these parts or even are just fine with them, that's great, and is an indication of the masculine support available within you to allow the feminine more room to play and expand. You may want to spend more time playing with some of the feminine aspects above, to nurture more of this energy in you.

- *How supported are you right now?*
  Again, notice what this brings up, and what you feel in your body.
  I've learned and seen in others that the more supported we are and feel, in all the ways – from financially to personal support for things like childcare or having a community and feeling like we have others to hold us and stand alongside – the more space there is for the feminine to flourish. If you don't feel supported, it's often easier to flip into the mind and start to try and think through things, falling back on the known and more ego-controlling way of doing and living. In this space, the feminine tends to withdraw and pull back, as there isn't the space for its energy to flow.

These are simply two prompts to get you tuning into this energy in your life right now. To begin to embody the masculine energy, which feels supportive and allows for the feminine to begin to come forth, here are a few qualities that you might want to start to lean into.

Foundations and grounding: Let yourself begin to root and sow seeds. It's these structures that take time but are also the base from which the feminine can feel held to flow and spread its magic. The feminine energy can take more time to reveal its magic, as it is not linear; it can be messy, unpredictable and super cyclical. But laying foundations and gathering support shows that what you are nurturing and growing might take time, but you are here to hold it until it is ready. Practically, this might mean getting support for an area that is not your strength or zone of genius. It may mean signing a contract or letting someone else know for accountability.

Devotion: Ultimately, this is about commitment and showing up. Showing up for whatever it is you are creating/bringing in. Showing up to co-create. Showing up in alignment with your guidance. Showing up through hard times, but honouring the process and cyclical parts of the feminine, knowing that showing up might mean different things at times.

Responsibility: This is the part where you take radical responsibility for whatever it is you are creating. This is owning up and claiming your part in its creation. Doing your work to align, to let go, to embody who you need to be to bring it into the physical. This is stepping up, stepping into and claiming your authentic power.

ON MOTHERS

I cannot not talk about Mothers when it comes to creation. Mothers are the ones that carry new life; they imprint upon it greatly and they have the power to change its trajectory through their own biology, genetics, care and holding in that important gestation period of womb-time. The role of the Mother is also generally the more feminine energy embodied that provides nurturing, care, and holding to bring up the young. Of course, the masculine energy plays a part here too, and I fully acknowledge and honour that there are men, non-binary, and transgender people in these roles.

Maybe you are a physical Mother to humans, fur babies, plants or something else. Perhaps you are a Mother who births businesses, books, creations, and/or more. You also have a biological Mother, even if not physically present, who carried you in her womb.

Mothers impact the way we create, what we create, how we create. On a biological level, their imprint leaves a mark as it's through them we receive half of our genetic DNA. We spend time in their wombs absorbing all of their feelings and emotions, taking on their experiences as if they were our own. The power of love and care we receive from our Mothers can literally change and reverse any damage that we may have received ancestrally.

To create a world that honours the whole, we have to restore our relationship with Mothers, and the damage that has been inflicted here for centuries. This is not to say we don't have to deal with the Father wounds, we absolutely do. But as the Mother energy is what carries us ALL, births us ALL, and provides the landscape for what we become, this is a good place to start.

Our relationship with our own Mother/s can play out in our lives, in how safe and supported we feel, how nurtured and cared for, accepted and whether we feel we belong. You likely also will have picked up behaviours and ways from your parent/s from how they were treated by their Mother/s. This in turn passes on to those we care for and/or parent. The cycle continues.

EMBODIED CREATION PROMPTS

* *What is/was your relationship with your Mother/s like?*
  If you don't have one, you could feel into any other Mother-like influences you may have had, such as a teacher or another family member. I also invite you to feel into what your time in the womb may have been like, simply trusting any intuitive feelings, thoughts and ideas that may arise.
* *What experiences and lessons did you gain from your Mother/s? How did they help you grow and evolve into who you are today?*
* *What more could you take from these experiences, even the painful/difficult ones?*
* *What do you need to hold, acknowledge, heal, and gently let go of to end any patterns or cycles that are no longer needed, to restore harmony and happiness?*

I have (and had) three official Mothers, plus many honorary ones, and I am sure there will be more. My biological Mother carried me, and birthed me into this world in India. My adopted mum (whom this book is in dedication to) brought me to Kenya with my dad, and then it was her time to pass on. I have a stepmother who has been one of my greatest teachers, which I only realised recently even though most of our life together has not been easy.

Much of my own journey of creation, has been centred around these three Mothers and their impact on my life. To align with the life I am creating, I have had to heal, acknowledge and hold, and let go of many, many, many stories and beliefs as well as trapped emotions I shut down and buried to protect myself.

This is only a small part of the depth of healing I have personally had to go into, and there are more layers and nuances. Whilst writing this book, as I shared in the introduction, I had a few months where there was nothing coming, and I was being called to do some deeper healing of my own. It was all centred around my relationship with my Mothers, and what I was still carrying that needed to be held and released.

I created many beliefs from my Mother passing on – that I wasn't enough, wasn't worthy, I wasn't wanted – stories I already had running deep from being given up for adoption. Her death of course impacted my whole family and so I created more beliefs based on, for example, my dad's reactions and his behaviours that followed. The ripple effect from situations that happen can truly play out in so many ways and continue to until they are healed.

Having a stepmother who for many years I didn't get on with created many more limiting and negative patterns and stories, again around being un-wanted and not belonging, feeling different from my stepsiblings. I then began to believe these stories even more and found more examples to affirm these beliefs throughout my life, such as not fitting in in university, feeling different to my work colleagues, never feeling enough. This continued until I began to do the healing and holding to let them go.

You see how the cycle continues and how we begin to create lives that reflect what we believe based on our experiences.

EMBODIED CREATION PROMPTS

- *What beliefs and stories have you picked up about yourself from your Mother/s?*
- *What have you made them mean about you?*

To start the healing process, I invite you to feel into whether these beliefs are true. They may feel very true to you; in which case, if you were your own parent, what would you say to yourself?

There's a process in the 'Limiting beliefs' part in the 'Creation blocks' section, which can support you further with belief work.

Additional practice

From the opposite side, a Shamanic practice I recently learned is to connect with the gifts you have received from this ancestral line. Take yourself on a journey to connect with the lineage of your biological Mother with the intention to learn, hear and/or receive, the qualities you may have inherited. You can also do it with your biological Father. As someone who is adopted, this was quite a profound practice, as I felt my intuition and compassion strongly from my Mother's side and my gentle strength from my Father's.

To do this, you can simply set the intention to be shown it, and then imagine yourself going down your Mother's lineage receiving the gifts, followed by your Father's. You could tune into your body and ask it to guide you, trusting whatever arises.

The Ancient Mother of all

Mother Earth is the great Ancient Mother of all.
She is here to guide us.
Hold us.
Nourish us.
Care for us.
Love us. Unconditionally.

She has deep wisdom and ancient knowledge to share with us.
She holds the answers for how to live a life that is in balance and harmony and that honours the whole.
She creates through seasons and cycles.

SEXUAL ENERGY IN CREATION

Sexual energy and creation are intrinsically linked. Sexual energy, without any of the conditioning, expectations, and meanings that society has laid upon it, is at its core pure life force energy, also known as Shakti. It is the beating pulse of all of life; it is wild, untamed, and the embodied expression of desire and passion that can create anything. It is pure creative power.

We are so out of touch with our sexual energy as we have learned to connect it primarily to the act of sex, which has become misunderstood, abused, sold, exploited, judged, feared and more. All sex is not like this, but a lot certainly is.

Many of us grew up feeling shame, guilt or other cultural conditioning around our sexual energy – and our desires and needs stemming from this energy – so we learned to shut it down and numb it or found ways to connect with it that became unhealthy and harmful to ourselves and others.

Our sexual organs are in our lower chakras – our root/base and sacral – so if we shut down our connection to this part of ourselves we begin to close off our connection to our life-force energy, and ability to feel safe and grounded in our creations and wholeness. This can lead to deep insecurities, seeking approval outside of yourself, not trusting in the flow of life, and an inability to bring that creative expression that you are here to embody.

Finding ways to re-connect with these parts of yourself can literally open you back up to your connection to this universal life-force energy, and your power as a creative being.

Inviting more pleasure into your life is a wonderful way to start connecting with this energy, as it reminds you of your needs and desires as a living being. This opens up the channels for more flow and re-connects you with your physical body in its magnificence.

In general, anything that helps clear stuck energy within your body and brings you deeply back into it (such as movement, massage, dancing), especially into your lower half, will support this.

Open yourself back up to your sexual energy. It is in you, it is a part of you, it is your birthright.

There are many wonderful resources available if you want to dive into this further as a way to harness your sexual energy, for yourself first and foremost, and to fuel into your creations. I have shared some resources at the end.

GETTING STARTED

HOW DOES THE ENERGY WANT TO COMMUNICATE WITH YOU?

How does the energy of what you are bringing through want to communicate with you?

Does it want you to sit down daily with it?
Does it speak to you through signs and symbols?
Does it want you to meditate with it?

Embodied Creation *unsurprisingly* only spoke to me when I was fully in my body. Some parts came when I was on walks, and later others through yin yoga. The seasons and cycles would only speak to me when I was outside connecting with the Earth or amongst the trees in my beloved forest.

Honour the connection, letting it flow and evolve.

If you ever feel stuck, return to nature. It is always there to hold you, guide you and take you by the hand.

How does the energy of what you are bringing through want to connect with you?

EMBODIED CREATION SHARE

'The soul of my business contacts me by making my right side tingle and fizz. It's like a knock on the door. 'May I come in?' It is respectful towards me and of my boundaries. It spreads across me like a white gentle light and energy.'
Grace Rose

EMBODIED CREATION PRACTICE

Write a letter to the energy of what you are being called to create, simply asking it to make itself known and whether it has anything it would like to share with you.

WHAT STAGE OF THE CREATION PROCESS ARE YOU IN?

Are your ideas forming, cocooning, growing, taking the time to fully form before being birthed into the physical? The space in between, where so much is happening – it's just not yet 'obvious'.

Are you birthing something right now? Taking grounded, inspired and aligned action – bringing your vision into reality.

Is there something you want to manifest into your life, perhaps a feeling or quality you want to embody, and you are at the early seed planting stages as you form your vision?

Maybe it's that you are in a personal inner winter, needing rest and replenishment, to take things slowly.

Perhaps you are coming out of a period of deep inner healing and are ready to begin seed planting and visioning, holding space for what wants to come through you.

Of course, we can be in different stages for different things.

My invitation to you is to allow yourself to be in whatever stage you are at.

When something is ready to be birthed, it will be. When something needs more time, pushing it will mean it's not ready. Remember to deeply honour your own inner season and self as a co-creator.

Our current society encourages constant growth and action, but this is not aligned with the feminine creative process or birthing of new ideas that will be sustainable.

EMBODIED CREATION PROMPTS

- *Where are you at? Tune into whatever it is you are co-creating and ask it.*
- *What season are you feeling internally right now?*
- *How can you honour the season you are in?*

CREATING JUST TO CREATE

Create without purpose.
Create without expectation.
Create just because.

Let the energy flow through you.
Let it move you.
Let it create a relationship with you.
Let it change you.

Let it come out in ways that are wild, unexpected, subtle, gentle, messy – whatever it wants to be.
Let yourself be led, guided, and held.
Let yourself create just for you.
Let it be just for you.

I highly recommend creating just to create as often as you feel called to do so, to tend to the flame of creation. Keeping it filled up, glowing, and alive with the current of life.

If you would like to join an online held space to create just for you every couple of months, take a look in the resources section at the end where I offer a low-cost space called 'A date to create' with all proceeds going to different organisations globally.

EMBODIED CREATION SHARE

Antonio is an artist, a creative, a singer and a healer. He used to create and sing just for himself as it connected him deeper within. It was always a healing experience and revealed the artist inside that could feel trapped at times. The dance between creating to make money and be productive and creating for himself came up in many of our conversations. During our time connecting he was called to lean back into creating for himself again and take his inner child on a playdate, to re-discover the magic of creation in the moment.

HONOURING YOUR SENSITIVITY IN CO-CREATION

The patriarchy doesn't honour the creative cyclical process. It wants to assert boundaries, order, control, put things in boxes. It wants to know what it will look like, right from the get-go. It wants it to stick to a schedule.

That's not how co-creation works.

It needs to be felt, seen and held in its essence.
It needs gentleness and allowing, space to form and grow in its own unique way.

Co-creation is about getting to know one another. It's about holding a deep, safe, womb- or cocoon-like space for your connection and own process to emerge. It's about honouring each other's needs as you find your way forward together. Knowing that it will guide you, but you also always have a say. You can ask it to slow down, clarify further, and support your needs too.

Honouring *both* of your sensitivity as you co-create together.

EMBODIED CREATION SHARE

Lilith was literally creating a baby inside of her. As a sensitive soul first and foremost, she was finding the system in Germany so hard, soul-less, cold and un-supportive to her needs. There was a distinct clinical feel and a complete lack of awareness around her anxiety and personal needs in the whole process of carrying a child. She was finding it hard to relax in appointments and her own health was suffering as her needs weren't being met. She even had to book private appointments with doctors who would allow her to have a say in what she needed. She eventually managed to find a nurse who used essential oils and aromatherapy, and this began to help a bit. She also had to clearly state her boundaries around what she was and wasn't willing to do or have done to her, and the space she needed.

What do you need to honour yourself as a sensitive co-creator?

CREATING SUSTAINABLY

Creating in a way that is sustainable and honours the whole can take time. The process also has to be sustainable, meaning that it needs to go deep with its roots, to lay strong, sturdy foundations.

It requires a willingness to do the work that will remove anything there already that may be damaging to the new seeds that are being planted. It needs to look at the beliefs, blocks, current systems, structures and ways in place that might need to be dismantled, held, and healed. It truly has to go deep to clear and till the soil for new shoots and waves of life to plant their tender selves there.

It needs to be fiercely protected whilst it is growing. It also needs to be tended to, nurtured, and fed, with time dedicated to its growth.

This could mean that you deeply look after yourself as the vessel for what wants to come through you and as the person who will be bringing or delivering it. This ensures that you are filled up and ready to play your part in its co-creation. It could be ongoing healing and support to let go of anything that might stop you from being all you can be when it is ready to be shared and make an impact.

It requires a new way of living, being and thinking. A way that honours nature, her rhythms and cycles, where there is rest and action, giving and taking, all combined in their unique harmony.

This is a reminder to tend to yourself, your needs and rhythms throughout the process.

INFUSE YOUR CREATION WITH THE QUALITIES OF THE ELEMENTS

Consider the qualities of each of the four main elements – Earth, air, fire and water – and how you can infuse them into your creation to support it with feeling balanced and whole.

Take a look at the list below and see what stands out to you, and whether you are missing qualities from one, or would like more from another.

Earth

Stable, grounded, nourished, prosperous, sustainable, dependable, fertile, secure.

Air

Magical, expansive, imaginative, harmonious, perceptive, intelligent, thoughtful.

Fire

Passionate, powerful, loving, activating, creative, strong, courageous, dynamic.

Water

Flowing, dreaming, healing, regenerating, unconditionally loving, receiving.

Are there any other qualities not listed that you would like to include?

WHAT'S THE INTENTION BEHIND YOUR CREATION?

As you have begun to dive into what moves you, what your heart wants to create alongside what is calling to come through, I invite you to really feel into the intention behind what you are co-creating.

Here are a few prompts to get you started.

- Where does it come from?
- What are its qualities?
- What is its purpose?
- Who is it for?
- What would you like people to feel when they receive it?

I also invite you to consider these questions as you tune in to the purpose of it.

- Are you creating from a place of wholeness?
- Are you creating to belong? To feel safe and secure?
- Are you creating from a place of lack or scarcity?
- Are you creating for yourself or for someone else?

EMBODIED CREATION SHARE

From the beginning with Embodied Creation, after hearing her first whisper and agreeing to be a co-creator, my intention was to help others with the process of creation for the highest good. Whilst I thought it was going to be about making manifesting available for all, it turned out to be co-creating with energies beyond us and deep care for the planet. Its qualities were always a connection to the feminine way, an honouring of seasons and cycles and creating a future that considers the whole. The purpose of the book and who it's for changed, as it's now more for people who want to create with the energies and for the good of the whole, which is sadly not everyone.

CREATION BLOCKS

This section includes support for some of the limiting beliefs and blocks that can rise on the journey of co-creation. It provides support to move through them, guiding you to hold and re-write them where possible, or go deeper if needed, leaning into the wisdom of the chakras and colour alchemy.

CONSCIOUS CREATION CAN BRING UP ALL THE THINGS

Feelings of not-good-enough-ness.
Feelings of not-worthy-enough.
The *who am I to have*? Question.

It may make you question your value.
It may make you question your desire.
It may make you question your deserved-ness.

It will shine a light on anything going on subconsciously in you that is out of alignment with what you are creating.

It may come up in the form of triggers.
It may come up as feelings and emotions, suddenly, out-of-nowhere.
It may come up as physical symptoms.
It may be something you hear, see or feel in your day-to-day life or interactions with others.

Although these 'irritations', scaling up to full-on WTF moments, may feel like they are here to side-line you, they are opportunities, ways for you to deeply hold yourself through them. Ways to give yourself what you need and step into your worthiness, your good-enough-ness, your power.
To show that you are damn-fucking-worthy.
To shift them. To change them. To release them from your field.
To ultimately align with what you are here to bring through.

ENOUGH

Until you believe you are 'enough', there will never be enough.
No amount of stuff will make you feel enough.
No amount of people can tell you that you're enough.
No number of qualifications can prove you're enough.

Until you believe you are 'enough', you will never feel enough.
You will never feel loved enough.
You will never feel worthy enough.
You will never feel beautiful enough.

No one can give you 'enough'.
It has to come from inside of you.

You have to know you are enough.
You have to feel enough.
You have to be enough.
You have to accept all of you.
Hold the parts that don't feel enough.
Forgive yourself.
Love yourself.
Your heart.
Your soul.
Your body.
Your mind.

You have to remember you are enough.
You are enough.
You are more than enough.

HOLDING AND HEALING YOUR-STORY

When it comes to creation, you may find yourself not fully aligning with what you are here to co-create. Even if you feel the energy of something strongly and are committed to bringing it through, you might come up against limiting beliefs and blocks, which on a subconscious level might be stopping you from taking action, feeling like 'who are you?' to bring the creation into the physical, or anything else that might be rising.

I go into limiting beliefs and blocks more in the next section, but alongside, or even prior to that, an exercise you can do which helps with letting go of past conditioning and beginning to heal some of the things you may have picked up in childhood, later life, or even other lives, is a deep dive into *your-story* – your own unique history – through your memories.

EMBODIED CREATION PRACTICE

Think back over all the memories in your conscious awareness (more will come up as you begin the process), and write down all the times something came up that might be impacting what you are creating at this time. All your memories that relate to what you want to create. This will call you to dig deep and really get under the surface.

For example, if you are co-creating a book, you might have memories around not doing well in an essay in school. You might remember being told your writing wasn't funny (and you are being called to write for comedy), you might have memories around coming last in a writing competition, etc. These memories link to writing in particular but as you dig deeper you might start to come upon memories which link to your value, what you believe you are capable of, what you feel the outcome might be based on past experiences, as well as other areas such as money. For example, you might think you don't have the money to self-publish, and this can bring up a whole load more stories around money from your past! This practice really can invite you to go deep into your-story, which as a plus benefits all areas of your life.

As soon as you feel you are at a place where you have written down as much as you can think of, you then need to go through each memory with the intention to heal it and release it. As a lot of these memories will likely be from your childhood, you may need to really hold yourself, or younger versions of yourself (see the 'Creating with your inner child' section for more guidance here) for what they experienced.

Then the idea is to forgive, release and be willing to see things differently, to create a NEW-story, for yourself and the part you will play as a co-creator. Please see the 'Limiting beliefs in creation' section for more support on how to do this, and if you need help, reach out to someone you trust.

EMBODIED CREATION SHARE

Autumn shares beautifully how she has been letting go, before being ready to move forward with what is calling to come through:

'You have to empty the vessel. If there was wine, and now you want to put tea in it, you first have got to empty everything out so that you don't get the residue and spoil whatever else you need to put in there. I think I finally came to that, which means that now I'm ready to move forward.'

LIMITING BELIEFS IN CO-CREATION

In our evolution and conditioning, we have learned to rely on our minds. We absolutely need our minds. They keep us safe – they remind us of what's dangerous and what's not. They let us know when there's something we need to escape from. They figure things out for us. They remember experiences. Plus so much more.

Unfortunately, our mind, or our ego part, hasn't evolved past being able to distinguish between real threats from our prehistoric times, e.g., from being eaten by a lion to the stress or feelings you might feel from modern-day living, which it then equates to being threats in the present and future.

It also has an incredible way of attaching meaning, which often turns into a belief/s, to experiences that might have happened in your life, which didn't feel particularly good. For example, you may have been laughed at or bullied in school for looking a certain way. This then may have translated into you believing that you weren't enough. Maybe you didn't do well in maths – this may then create a belief around being bad with numbers and you'll do all you can to avoid them. There are so many examples and ways we can create beliefs attached to situations and experiences, especially as a sensitive person.

We might also create beliefs based on what we see others doing, what others say to us, especially people in positions of authority or that we look up to, such as parents, caregivers, teachers, other family members and friends.

When it comes to creation, especially embodied creation, the main area that can likely come in and trip you up is the limiting beliefs that come from your memories. These are the thoughts, patterns, and beliefs that rise which tell you that you can't have what you desire. *Who are you to have or do xyz? What makes you so special? You aren't worthy of that.* They may reinforce why you don't really want what you think you do, as something bad may happen.

Our minds are incredibly powerful and can cause us to feel a certain way in our bodies, which can have both a positive and negative impact. For creation to be embodied, you actually need to feel the desired feeling (how you will feel when you get what you desire) in your body before it becomes a physical reality. If our thoughts are making us feel out of alignment, un-worthy, un-deserving, fearful (or something else) on the inside, we literally won't be able to create what we desire, as there will be a misalignment going on. Think of it like the positive and negative charges on a magnet repelling one another – what we say we want and what we feel on the inside aren't matching up.

As you do this work, you will find some core beliefs begin to rise as ones that have been conditioned into you strongly and are playing out in multiple areas in your life. There will also be nuances, layers and threads to them.

You'll also happen upon others that will rise as you begin this journey of conscious co-creation.

The beliefs that rise for you will be unique to you. Your history, background, stories, conditioning, culture, experiences, etc. So, it's up to you to do the digging with conscious awareness of what rises for you as you begin to vision and feel into what you are creating.

Here are some of the main things I have come across that rise as beliefs. They very often tie into issues around self-worth and fearing the loss of something.

- I am not worthy of it.
- I don't deserve it.
- I am not enough.
- Who am I to have/do/be xyz?
- Something bad will happen if I get/am/do xyz.
- I'll lose something or have to give something up, such as my freedom and time.
- It will be too hard.

Here is an example around beliefs being created, to show how easily we can create them and why this might then be a reason deep down inside we don't actually want what we think we do, or perhaps don't want to be the one to bring it through.

From my own life growing up in Kenya I saw and felt the contrasts between wealth and poverty hugely and I felt a lot of guilt around having more than so many. I saw my parents always paying for everyone and so started to associate having money with being the one to always pay and be responsible for others, no matter the situation.

Belief created: Having money is a burden and an obligation to be responsible for others. I also took this further to mean if I get successful from the creations I bring through, I'll have to be more responsible for others, and I like my freedom.

To understand the belief that you have created, you can ask the question 'What did I make this situation mean?' – this will usually give a good indication of your underlying belief.

Another way is to tune into what you are being called to create and see what rises as you connect to deeply having and experiencing it.

When beliefs come up, the next step is starting to see where they came from, then heal, release, forgive and let them go before beginning to re-write them. Here is a process you can use for all beliefs.

1. Start to become aware of all the thoughts and ideas coming up telling you that you can't have/embody/bring through what you desire, and the beliefs that you have created. Here are some questions to help you tune into the underlying belief that might be playing out.

    *   Why don't you actually want what you say you do?
    *   What do you fear you will lose if you get what you desire?
    *   What fears are rising?
    *   What bad things do you think will happen if you get what you desire?
    *   What are all the reasons coming up that tell you that you can't have it/why it's not possible for you?

- What would having/receiving this mean for you?
- How would it change your life negatively? (You may not think it will on the surface, but as you dig into it, I am sure you will come up with some reasons.)

2. Now, looking at everything you wrote down, ask yourself, 'Is it true?' (It very rarely is, and if there's an element of truth in there, it is likely not the whole truth and can be shifted, or perhaps you are here to create a new way!)

3. Start to re-write these beliefs. Hold and heal anything that needs to be. Where did it come from? Often we need to go back to childhood and comfort that younger version of ourselves, letting them know that it's okay and even doing some re-parenting. It might also be ancestral, from a past life or conditioning, in which case you may need some other support to let it go. There are some resources for this at the end.
Spend time forgiving or releasing anything or anyone that played a part in this belief being formed, for your own sake. Set an intention to release and let those beliefs go, even if it feels like you don't know how yet – the inspiration will come.

4. Connect with these new truths/possibilities and really spend time embodying each one of them wholly – connecting to and feeling it in all of your being.

More 'stuff' may arise as you begin to connect with new truths/possibilities – these are all the things you need to continue to work through.

EMBODIED CREATION SHARES

As Sophia was connecting to a vision she had of creating a sanctuary to share and support others with her wisdom around plants, blocks arose around why she didn't actually believe it was possible for her, even though she felt the energy of it very strongly. 'It's too big a project, it costs too much, I don't have a steady secure fixed income – I have to have a steady job first, I can't do this alone, this isn't for spiritual people like me, I don't deserve this, I'm too old for this, things like this don't just happen – you have to work for it ...'

Antonio was being called to create a music single, and as he connected with it being a reality a block came up before he had even begun, around not wanting people to think he is greedy if he made money from it. As he dug into it, he felt there could be something related to his culture and the beliefs embedded in the consciousness. There's a lot of discrepancy between the rich and the poor where he lives in Brazil, as well as a lot of corruption and injustice, which he grew up hearing about from society, family, the media, etc.

He recognised that this is likely in his subconscious, as on a conscious level he knows that having more for himself and/or earning from his art and business would allow him to create more and help support himself, his family and friends and the collective.

This is the new empowering truth he is now tuning into.

CREATING WITH YOUR INNER CHILD

Younger you, or younger versions of you, come up a lot on the journey of creation – bringing your desires into the physical.

For many, younger you is the one that is creative, that believes in magic, that came into this world knowing that anything is possible, that creates just by being them. Then somewhere along the line, you might have been told to stop dreaming, stop believing in some way, and to get serious and live the life laid out for you by society, your parents, etc.

So, forming a new relationship with younger you is essential to the journey of creation for a couple of reasons:
Firstly, to heal, hold and release the blocks and beliefs that you might have created as a result of what you experienced, so that you can create new truths and beliefs that feel good in your body and are a vibrational match for what you desire. Young you has to get on board with this to be able to deeply embody your new beliefs, or at least this is the case for most, which we went into in the 'Healing and holding YOUR-story' section.
This also allows you to re-connect with the power of creation and 'creating just because you can' that often exists in a younger version of you.

In my own journey of creation, connecting with younger me formed the majority of my inner work, to let go of the beliefs that were weighing me down and stopping me from believing I could actually bring through and embody/have what I desired to create.

Rather than connecting to just one younger version of me, I found that there were younger versions of me at different ages where I had various things still playing out on a subconscious level in my reality. For example, 7-year-old me was the go-getter and liked to be seen, so she wanted to charge ahead. 11-year-old me had a lot to say about her self-worth. 14-year-old me needed to be told she was worthy and beautiful exactly as she was. 21-year-old me needed reassurance and to know it would all be okay. These contrasting parts within me could be both a support and something that stopped me.

EMBODIED CREATION SHARE

Here is a little of what 11-year-old me had to say when I was launching a programme all tied into chakras and business blocks:
'Who am I to do this? Why do I get to share, create and do business in a way that feels good in my heart when so many have to work hard and struggle to get by? Nobody will want it anyway. It won't help people, it won't offer enough value.'

As I got to the root of these thoughts, they tied into what I felt my worth and value was as a child. I went into experiences feeling un-wanted and un-loved, and like I didn't matter. So I had to do a lot of holding of younger me, before I could begin to write a new, more empowering story, that looked something like this.

'You have so got this! You are here to create a new way. A way that feels good to you and the people you are sharing it with. You know this "work" works. You know it's needed. People have had amazing results with it, yourself included. You are here to do it in a new way. It is so needed!'

EMBODIED CREATION PRACTICE

If this resonates I invite you to spend time with yourself at different ages. Feel into what age might be good to start. If you have them, you can also look at photographs of yourself at the different ages, which is incredibly powerful. You can then speak or write to this younger version of yourself and support yourself as needed. There are some resources at the end to help you with this.

WHAT DO YOU BELIEVE YOU ARE WORTHY OF?

If you grew up in struggle and living hand-to-mouth, wondering where the next paycheck is coming from, you may not believe you are worthy of more than this.

If you had parents that didn't have time for you, who missed seeing your proud moments in school, you may believe you don't deserve to have anyone there for you, or you won't have anyone to share future proud moments with, so what's the point.

If you felt different to the other kids and were the one left out, you may not believe you can ever have true friendships.

'What do you believe you are worthy of?' is one of, if not THE, most important questions when it comes to aligning with what you desire to create. What you believe you are worthy of will determine what you will allow into your life moving forward.

To co-create a reality that considers the whole, you have to know, believe and embody your worthiness.

EMBODIED CREATION PROMPT

* *What are you still holding on to that is telling you that you are not worthy?*

I invite you to feel into this question and allow what wants to come up for you. Know that this might take time and some deep inner work. Hold yourself through what rises, ask for help and guidance if needed, and let the answers come to you.

COLOUR AND THE CHAKRAS FOR HEALING BELIEFS AND BLOCKS

Working with and leaning into the power of the chakras and colour psychology is something I infuse into all my work and offers. My book *Embodied Business* is all about clearing, releasing, and healing blocks in alignment with the chakras, blocks that might be holding you back in some way from being all you are here to be (whilst it's aimed at empath entrepreneurs, many of the principles apply no matter what you do).

As you begin to consciously create, if you find you come up against limiting beliefs and/or blocks that go deep, it might not be as simple as being able to just write new beliefs, as I shared in the previous section. You might need other support, holding and healing to get to the root cause, to truly acknowledge what was experienced (in this lifetime and others) and provide the necessary healing for you to move through it, and get behind a new, more empowering belief. This has certainly been the case for me.

If you do find that you can't get to the bottom of a block, you can try feeling the energy of the block and asking what colour it is, then based on that, take a look below to see what it might be about. This can help to start getting the energy moving and for you to perhaps figure out where it came from, to do the necessary healing, holding and releasing. You can do this with regression work, which I highly recommend as a powerful way to heal and let things go.

Here are what certain colours (from the Colour Mirrors system) can suggest you might need, as well as the chakras they are typically in and some of the past lives the colours can suggest. Please also check out the resources at the end, as they might support you.

Earth star chakra (copper)

Issues around grounding, feeling safe to be on Earth.
Past life/lives: African.

Root/base chakra (red)

Issues around victimhood, judgements, martyrdom, struggle, survival, anger, pain, pleasure.
Past life/lives: Russian, Chinese, feast or famine issues, survival.

Sacral chakra (orange)

Issues around trauma, creation, bliss and manifestation, pleasure, sexuality, orgasm.
Past life/lives: Tibetan, Native American, Hindu nun or monk.

Solar plexus chakra (yellow)

Issues around power, control, worthiness, being you, connecting with your inner child, joy and magic.
Past life/lives: Egyptian, Mayan, Inca, sun god worship. With green – Cathar.

Heart chakra (green)

Issues around boundaries, truth and wisdom, feeling loved, safe and accepted.
Past life/lives: European persecution/inquisition. With violet – witch burnings. Fear around being a healer.

Higher heart chakra (turquoise)

Issues around oneness, conscious creation, flow, trust.
Past life/lives: Atlantis.

Throat chakra (blue)

Issues around expressing and asking for your desires, speaking it into existence.
Past life/lives: Biblical, Israel.

Third eye chakra (indigo)

Issues around visioning and connecting with your intuition, control, structures and authority.
Past life/lives: Mystery schools, priest/priestess teachings, initiations.

Crown chakra (purple)

Issues around receiving divine guidance, grief, depression, judgement, spirituality, being a healer.
Past life/lives: Catholic connections.

Soul star chakra (magenta)

Issues around alignment with your soul plan and purpose, co-creation, separation, over-giving, burnout.
Past life/lives: Japanese.

Once your chakras are feeling aligned, you can tune into their potency to help you create. This is how I see their power in creation.

The chakras in creation

Earth star – nourishment and grounding, coming back to our Earth Mother.
Base/root – feeling safe, held and at home here on Earth.
Sacral – pleasure and receiving, tuning into your sexual energy as creative life force.
Solar – authentic power and knowing you are more than enough.
Heart – love and compassion for all, creating from this space.
Higher heart – trusting that your creations will have an impact even if it doesn't seem like it now.
Throat – speaking it into existence, the power of your voice.
Third eye – visioning a future for yourself and the good of the whole.
Crown – following the guidance that comes and co-creating with what you are bringing through.
Soul star – trusting your soul's path and what/who you are here to be.

LET IT BE EASY

We make it so hard. So many of us have been conditioned to think that hard work is the way to prove yourself, to get things done, to make things happen, to earn what you desire.

If things come easily there could be a feeling of judgement or resentment from others, whether perceived or real. Life isn't fair, so why does it come easily to some and not others. As a sensitive soul, you don't want to be that person whom everything comes easily to, as you may feel separate from so many, like you don't belong, and you don't deserve to have good experiences and things without having to do much.

How does all the struggle feel?
How does having to prove yourself feel?

Not very good, I bet! In fact, it's pretty damn exhausting.

What if it could just be easy? What if you could let yourself be the magical, magnetic light that you are and for things to come to you like a moth to a flame? Letting yourself create, receive and live in alignment with the rhythm of life.

Think of all that you could do for yourself, for others, for this world, if you allow it to be easy. Just because it's hard for so many, it's time to start creating a new way. It's time to let yourself be different and step into ease and flow, so that you can truly bring all of you to the table. Your heart, your compassion, your empathy, your kindness.

When you are stuck in struggle, pushing, forcing, striving, it shuts down the parts of you that need space and gentleness to thrive. And the world needs these gifts badly, dear sensitive one.

EMBODIED CREATION PROMPT

- *What would it take for you to let it be easy?*

ASK FOR AND/OR FIND THE HELP YOU SPECIFICALLY NEED

When it comes to this work, healing past traumas, letting go and holding what needs to be acknowledged and released, my experience that I share about and from is going to be just that – MY experience. What I share may relate, of course, but at the end of the day, your lived experience, your story, your ancestry, and your traumas are going to be unique to you.

There is always help available that can support you with your individual situation. Maybe it's an area that I don't mention at all, as it's not something that comes up for me. Maybe it's something that you keep coming up against and can't find a way through.

If you aren't sure where to start, get online and find the resources YOU need: support groups, teachers and others who may have similar lived experiences. Ask for guidance from the unseen (God, Divine, Universe – whatever you believe in), and let it come to you in ways that you might not expect.

Always ask for the help that you need. There is always a way through.

THE SEASONS OF CREATION

The seasons of creation: spring, summer, autumn/fall and winter, the seasons through which Mother Earth creates, includes guidance, prompts, stories, inspiration and nourishment from nature. These seasons are mirrored in our own bodies (for those of us that do – or have in the past – menstruate), as well as in the lunar cycle.

This section invites you to tune into the wisdom of each season to co-create what you are calling to bring through.

SPRING

Yang

Waxing moon

Element – Air

Chakras – higher heart, throat, third eye, crown, soul star (not limited to these)

Qualities – visioning, seed planting

SEASONS OF CHANGE

The transition seasons of spring and autumn/fall can bring up anxiety and a tired but wired feeling, amongst other things. It's the shift in energy, the change from the solidness of winter and the strength of summer. Although these seasons are also of course changing, there is something in them that feels stable. You know where you are at. And for most of us, creatures of habit and consistency, there is comfort in that.

When and if you feel your body pulling at you in this season of change, it's inviting you to slow down. Be more mindful, and drop into the sanctuary of yourself. This is where the calm amidst the chaos is. This is where you need to be for the magic to unfold. Your body is telling you it's not quite time yet. Honour the season you are in, and let your creation cocoon some more, while you tend to your body, mind and soul.

Spring Cleaning

Whilst I see autumn/fall as the season for letting go and releasing blocks and beliefs that are not serving you and your creation, spring is also about releasing any stagnancy that may have built up. Checking in with what's going on under the surface and doing some cleaning and clearing.

This could be decluttering physically to make space. It could be seeing what beliefs and ideas are coming up for you that are not helpful for you and your creation, then supporting yourself to let them go. It could be releasing something such as a habit or pattern, or even a person, that you know is not aligned with what you are bringing through.

Embodied Creation Prompt

* *What is this season calling you to clear to support the full, grounded presence of what you are creating?*

STEPPING INTO SPRING

Spring is here.
The energy is rising.
I feel the noticeable shift and bubbling inside.
The part of me that's been conditioned by school, work, society, wants to leap into everything.
Start taking action, hard and fast.

But no.

My body is telling me to ease my way in.
Like tender shoots, delicately beginning to emerge, their fragility still apparent, I am being called to dip my toe out cautiously, tentatively, gently.
It's not the time to give, plan too much, overdo it.

Now is the time to soak in the space of possibility.
The in-between where universes are formed.
To lean into the spark of ideas and inspiration brewing.
Let them grow another layer, develop a little further, before they are ready for me to play my part in co-creation.

For now I must hold my vision strong, feel it, believe it, know it, embody it.
Be patient.
Trust in the deep magic of embodied creation.

WHAT ARE YOU BEING CALLED TO CO-CREATE RIGHT NOW?

There's an energy rising, you can feel it in your bones.
It may start as a whisper, calling your attention in fleeting moments.
It may get louder, bolder and strong.
Until eventually it can be ignored no longer.

It's the spark of a new creation.
The life force of something that wants to 'be'.
The energy of what the Earth is calling for.
A knowing in your heart that you are here to bring it in.

To let it guide you.
Let it form and take shape.
To co-create with it.
As you do your part to make it physical.

As you sit with this energy.
Feel it deeply.
Get to know it.
Let it take as long as it wants.
Give it time to make itself known.
What are its qualities?
What is its essence?
Does it have a purpose?
Where does it come from?
Really deeply feel it.

What are you being called to create right now?
Honour what wants to come through you.

EMBODIED CREATION SHARE

Before Nicola (my publisher) became a writing mentor and publisher, she connected with a powerful vision where she saw a group of women around her. Each one was carrying a drop of silver liquid. One after another, each of the women stepped forward with her droplet and together they formed a beautiful, silver pool. During the vision, she heard the words, 'The power to move mountains'.

At the time, she had no clue how that vision would manifest. But looking back, she can see that this was setting the scene for The Unbound Press and the community that's grown around it. Each silver drop is a book and when they come together, they have the power to move mountains, change the world and be part of birthing New Earth.

TRUST WHAT IS COMING THROUGH

Trust the spark, the inspiration, the idea.
If it has come to you, it's yours to bring through.
You don't need to question it.
Get another qualification, certification, seal of approval.
You know enough. You are enough.
Let it lead you, guide you and support you.

All you need to do is trust what is coming through.

WHAT SEEDS ARE YOU PLANTING?

What are you being called to create right now?

Take a moment and tune into your heart to hear its whispers.

Get clear on 'why' you want it.
What will it bring to your life?
Who else will it serve?
What will it bring to the planet?
Deeply connect to this

EMBODIED CREATION SHARES

Vanessa has this vision to create spaces that help people be their best selves. Whether that's clients, her family, her team, or students, it all comes down to creating an environment where everyone feels seen, heard, nurtured, and supported. From there they can be fully themselves.

Jaideep wants to cultivate more joy in his life and in the lives of his family, friends and community. Happiness is the key feeling he seeks daily, which guides his actions.

TENDING TO THE FLAME

The new, spring energy of creation has a dance in its step, and the playful curiosity of an excited child whispering at your ear, calling for your attention, wanting to be out in the world.

There's also a tentativeness to it. It needs to be kept close. It needs to feel safe and supported. It is still young, fresh and growing.

This energy is still getting to know you, and you it, so for now I invite you to keep it close.
It needs holding and tending to, like the spring buds, delicate as they begin to emerge.
Feed it, water it, nourish and nurture it. Hold it safely to grow, just a little bit more.
Keep tending to the flame, the essence, the life force of your creation.

Just like the soil is prepared for seeds to be planted, tending to this energy calls for you to tend to YOU. So you can be the person who brings forth this creation, the person who is ready to receive it in the physical.

EMBODIED CREATION PROMPTS

* *Are you ready for what is coming through? What do you need? How can you support yourself in this moment?*
  For example, do you need to eat healthy, nourishing foods to energise yourself even more, and be the vessel for what you are being called into? Do you need to reach out for help from someone in some way?
* *Is there anything else that your creation might need, that you can begin to lay the foundations for?*
  Perhaps there are some systems that you need to put in place. Maybe you need to get support in another way to hold your creation. Perhaps you can spend time visualising filling up the energy of your creation with light – breathing life force into it. Connect with what it will need when it's here, and let it guide you.

YOU GET TO CHOOSE

It's so easy to just get on with it.
Do what you are told.
Live the life handed to you.
Do what everyone else does, because that's the norm.

But what if that's not really what you want?
Take a moment, connect within, is it?
You get to choose.

It's so easy to think we have to do the 'right' thing.
Say the 'right' thing.
Be the 'right' person.

But what if that's not really what you want?
Take a moment, connect within, is it?
You get to choose.

EMBODIED CREATION PRACTICE

Take a moment, many moments in fact, throughout your day and tune in to your truth.
The wisdom of your body knows. What do you choose?

EMBODIED VISIONING

What is your vision?

What does it look, feel, sound like?

What qualities does it hold?

Who is the person you need to become/be/embody for your vision to be here right now?

How does that version of you show up?

What do they think, feel, say?

What do they do differently from what you do now?

Is there anything they don't do that you do?

What is their energy like?

If you could describe them in one word, what would it be?

How will it feel when your desire shows up in your life?

What will you be doing/thinking/being?

As you connect to your vision, moving closer to embodying it, you open yourself to receiving the guidance for what wants to come through that's aligned with it.

EMBODIED CREATION PROMPT

What one action step can you take to be that version of you in this moment? E.g., start to show up in a different way. Commit to something that will support you to feel the way this version of you does. Let something go, such as a habit that this version of you doesn't have.

EMBODIED CREATION PRACTICE

Write a story about this version of you living in the vision you desire. Describe it vividly, in detail. Tune into your senses: what does it feel like, taste like, smell like, look like, etc.? Then read it aloud, perhaps even record yourself and listen to it when you feel called to (first thing in the morning and last thing at night are often powerful times for this).

You could alternatively, or additionally, draw a picture/create a collage of this vision with you in it, and stick it up to serve as a powerful visual reference.

EMBODIED CREATION SHARE

For a long time, I deeply felt that I am here to help others, to support them to create change in their lives, to be all they can be, so we look out for one another and our home, Earth. But for many years I was going through a lot of my own stuff – drinking and eating to numb all I was feeling, working in jobs that I resented (at the time – in hindsight I am truly grateful for each one and what it gave me), internally loathing myself and much more. Not embodying the person I felt deep down inside I truly was or could be.

Without knowing this is what I was doing I began connecting to a vision of me helping others, writing books, creating art, helping others through my work – even though I didn't know what that specifically was. I felt that version of me and knew I'd be living it one day.

Very slowly, over the course of at least a decade, things began to re-align and I can now say I am starting to live that vision. It began with me looking after myself on a whole new level, acknowledging, healing and holding my past traumas. Getting support and letting the layers shed away. I went back and forth, it was messy, cyclical, spiralling.

I have let that vision pull me through. I have taken it step by step. As I've done this, I've truly allowed myself to align with it, and it's only just the beginning! I can't wait to see where it takes me. I wanted what I have today back then, but I can see now that I wasn't ready for it at that time in my life. There was a whole other journey I needed to go through, and I am so grateful I did.

KEEP GROUNDING YOUR VISION

Just like newly planted seeds must grow strong roots before they rise above ground, you too must ground your vision deeply into the holding and support of Mother Earth before the action above ground can be taken.

This is where it creates its stable foundation. This is where it becomes grounded and solid.

EMBODIED CREATION SHARE

At the end of 2020, I started getting the glimmers of a group programme I wanted to bring into the world. It felt like it was going to be connected to my book Embodied Business, which is all about clearing, releasing and healing chakra blocks on the entrepreneurial journey, but I wasn't exactly sure what it was, when it wanted to come, etc.

So I began connecting to this energy through meditations and visualisations, committing to do so every day for a month. At first, I was taken to this landscape that looked and felt like the desert. As I waited there, I saw this cocoon-spaceship flying over the mountains towards me, and then it came and landed.

It was there for a few days, not moving, not doing anything and I just had to be there with it, present, allowing it to guide me. After a few days of this it started to unfurl and open and eventually this tree started to take shape, but only at night, with coloured fruits in the different chakra colours growing on it.

I kept connecting to it, asking it what it needed, as I can be quite an impatient person at times, wanting to get on with stuff. I kept asking if there was any action I could take, and what did it look like as I wanted to know and get it out into the world.

But for about two weeks (which actually is super fast – I've had other creations take months), it just wanted to be nurtured.

It needed sunshine, water, minerals and nutrition. So this is what I gave it in my connections, and the 'action' guidance I was given was to nurture myself so that I too could feel strong, nourished and supported to hold the space for what this was going to turn into.

It eventually gave me the structure of the programme, and practical ways to share it, but the main thing I got from that experience was to focus on its energy.

As I tended to it daily, it began to grow and reach outwards, and the fruits turned into beautiful homes that looked like mini tree-house-nests for the people that were being called to land and go through the programme. My job was to energetically support those spaces to feel as nourishing and magnetic as possible.

As we moved towards the launch of the programme, I saw this alchemical, magical energy which looked a bit like galaxies of stars and colours coming together, so this is what I connected to and grounded daily as I was sharing about it and inviting people in.

For someone who loves colour, creativity and fun, it was such an aligned way to launch something and reach the people who needed and wanted it. It showed me that this way also works and that creating is so magical!

VISUALISATION TO GROUND THE ENERGY

I invite you to read through these words first, then either close your eyes or lower your gaze and follow the guidance to ground the energy of your vision.

Imagine a light at your root, your base chakra and begin to bring the vision of your creation into this light. Whatever this looks or feels like to you, imagine it coming into this portal. Hold it here and breathe into it, letting it expand as much as it wants. Then when you feel ready, begin to draw it down into your Earth star chakra a few inches beneath you in the ground. Feel the energy going down, breathing into it, letting it become bigger, spreading out. Allowing it to root and ground deeply.

Keep holding it here, breathing into it as it earths and becomes more stable. Connect to it as often as you can and remember to have patience. This part is so important.

COMMIT TO BRINGING YOUR CREATION TO LIFE

It's time to whole-heartedly, full-bodily, soul-fully, commit to your creation.

Commit to what it calls of you.
Commit to it even when and if it gets hard.
Commit to showing up.
Commit to holding the vision, allowing it to flow if needed.
Commit to looking after yourself to be all you can be to co-create with your creation's energy.
Commit to getting support when you need it.
Commit to trusting the process.
Commit to taking aligned action.
Commit to letting it all go if called to.
Commit to resting.
Commit to letting it breathe.

Commit to birthing it with the highest intention.

CREATING FLOW THROUGH MOMENTUM

Sometimes we can sit with it all swirling around for ages.
Wanting to know before we begin, before we do anything.

Start taking action to see how the pieces will begin to fit together.
Allowing what wants to fall away and what wants to come in.

Take that first step, just that little one.
Don't overthink it.
Try to figure it all out.
See the whole picture.

Just take that first step.
Let the energy begin to flow through.
As it forms into the physical.
Letting it lead.
Letting it be what it will be.

EMBODIED CREATION PROMPT

*   *What one action step are you being called to take to co-create?*

BUTTERFLY MAGIC

While writing this section, connecting deeply to my own inner spring, I was doing as I felt intuitively and sitting, being with myself in the spaces between clients, calls and work. As I did, an orange butterfly came and landed on my toe. It stayed there, exploring, moving on to the next and the next. For a while it circled around me, then kept coming back to rest and walk over my toes.

It felt like such a beautiful confirmation of the power of the spring energy. Playful, dancing, with pockets of rest. Simply being. Present. Taking the time to stop and smell the roses and being rewarded with such moments of magic.

I had been asking for a sign from the Universe that all is well and to trust in what is coming through to share in the book, and this certainly was it for me.

Sometimes we need these little extras, these synchronicities, that give hope, that help us to keep going. To lean into another way, to remind us that we are on track.

Writing in this way has asked me to trust on another level, to let myself be guided, and this is what we are being called into, deeply, as we create a world that moves into a new way of being and living.

LISTEN CLOSELY

As spring softly turns into summer, the energy begins to shift once again.
There's an air of magic, flow and ease, with a good dash of pleasure that wants to come in.

You are being invited to stop and listen, feel, allow it.
Take a moment to muse with nature and let her guide you.

EMBODIED CREATION PRACTICE

Spend some time in your nearest natural surroundings, if weather permits (otherwise you can imagine or visualise it). Whilst there, I invite you to begin to speak to nature with a clear intention to receive guidance around what you are being called to co-create. Let the answers come to you through messages – what you see, hear, feel – and trust whatever that may be.

SUMMER

Yang

Full moon

Element – Fire

Chakras – sacral, solar plexus, heart (not limited to these)

Qualities – manifesting, pleasure, play

WHAT GIFTS DO YOU BRING JUST BY BEING YOU?

At your core, your centre, are the qualities that were imbued into your being – mind, body and soul, when you came onto this Earth.

They are the parts of you that you embody without even trying.
They are the things that you find easy to live and share with others.
You might not even notice them.
You might mistakenly think everyone has them.
You might take them for granted.
You might reduce their importance and potential impact.

But these are your YOU-ness, your essence, a part of your contribution to the whole.
They are so magical, magnificent and miraculous.
They are what the world needs right now.
They are your thread in the great tapestry of the new earth.

It's time to claim them, own them and bring them.
What gifts do you bring just by being you?

EMBODIED CREATION PRACTICE

I invite you to write a list of the gifts you bring just by being you, and practice living (noticing how they contribute to others and yourself) at least one of them every single day.

LEANING INTO PLEASURE

Pleasure is a gateway to deep nourishment which supports the seeds of creation. It is intimately connected to your sacral and root chakras, which are the seat of creation, and the portal from where new, embodied creations will spring. On a biological level, creation of human babies (without medical intervention) usually also begins with pleasure. It goes without saying that pleasure and creation go hand-in-hand.

At the beginning of 2021, I was reflecting on pleasure, and I realised I didn't know where in my life I was feeling or receiving pleasure, aside from food. And after having Covid I didn't have full taste for months, so that wasn't even appealing anymore.

So, I challenged myself to write a list of 30 things that gave me pleasure and committed to a daily practice of doing at least one thing, which at the time of writing has been going on for over a year now.

I forgot how much fun it is to feel pleasure.

We have been so conditioned to think of pleasure as a luxury and something that we have to earn or work hard for, but actually by incorporating more mindful pleasure into our lives, the more magical life gets as we truly begin to embody these delicious feelings. Reminding us that life is to be enjoyed, and we deserve to enjoy it. Every. Single. Day.

Here are some of my pleasure practices, which might inspire you and show that it doesn't have to cost much or take much time, unless you want it to.

Giving myself a salt scrub in the shower and having glowing, baby soft smooth skin as a result; fresh sheets when I want them (yes, I do change my sheets regularly but there's something sooo pleasurable about doing this just because you want them); painting to enjoy the colours; walks amongst the trees; reading erotica;

hot baths; self-massage; self-pleasure; deep yin yoga; staring at the trees; napping; cooking something new; watching old-school romantic comedies that make me feel like a teenager all over again; eating chocolate; taking a few minutes to lie on the ground; feel the hot skin warming my bones (oh the benefits of life in the tropics); walking to a nearby river and listening to the flow of water; closing my eyes and listening to the different bird sounds; watching butterflies dance from flower to flower; having deep conversations about shit that matters (I don't do small talk) with people who also like to dive right in; my morning coffee.

I've also noticed that the more pleasure I feel, the more I let go, get in my body and the more I connect with the truth of what I am here to create, as well as my pure creative energy.

EMBODIED CREATION SHARE

As Sophia connected to the intention to bring more pleasure into her life, she received the following guidance, practices which all deeply honoured her womb as the seat of creation: massage hawthorn and rose oils onto her womb; play sounds like singing bowls near her womb; place crystals or stones on her womb; bless the womb; make womb waters using flowers and then massage them on to the womb; make womb wraps – using different coloured cloths wrapped around her womb space; create womb art – using earth/mud/flowers on her body; sing to her womb.

EMBODIED CREATION PRACTICE

What brings you pleasure?
I invite you to consciously explore your senses. Each and every one, from your smell to your taste, touch, sight, sound, and feelings.
I invite you to set an intention to receive the guidance that will support you to create more pleasure in your life.

EMBODYING AND MAGNETISING YOUR VISION

Here is a short visualisation you can do in the summer phase (or whenever you feel called) to enhance the energy of your creation.

You can read the words below and then, using them as guidance, follow them with your vision. Or you can find a meditation recording of them called 'Magnetising your vison' in the resources section at the end.

Connect with the vison of what you desire as a ball of energy.
Bringing it down to your Earth star chakra, a few inches below you in the ground.
Feel the energy there, and let its roots bury deep into the fertile soils of Gaia.
Then bring the energy up into all your chakras, your root, your sacral, solar plexus, heart, higher heart, throat, third eye and crown.
As it connects with each one, feel it sending a magnetic sonar out, lighting up your entire being and field around you.
Hold this.
Lie in this.
Bask in this.
Let it light up every cell in your body.
Know that what you desire is coming.
Let yourself receive it by deeply feeling that it's here already.

OWN WHAT YOU ARE BEING CALLED INTO

You've got to own what you are being called into.
The person your creation is calling you to be.
These creations that come through you often need you to embody a different energy, essence and way.

They are an activation.
A portal.
An invitation.

They will call you to step up.
To own your power, your wisdom, your truth.
They will draw you into your next level.
Becoming that version of you who can hold them.

They will live through you.
They will move through you.
They will change you irreversibly.

You've got to own it.
You've got to step into it.
Be, live, and become it.
I invite you to own the shit out of what you are being called into.

Aligned Action can Happen Fast

As the yang energy of spring and summer takes over, there are times when the aligned guidance to do something comes in thick and fast.

Action that propels you towards your vision and fulfils your part in its co-creation.
Perhaps it's showing up.
Maybe it's clearing and/or healing the blocks or limiting beliefs that are rising.
It could be doing something practical.

Surfing this wave of momentum can feel exhilarating and intense all at the same time.

Be careful not to burn out. To not overdo it.
Ultra-self-care is essential.

Lean on our Earth Mother when needed.
Bury your roots into her embrace, and let her ground you, hold you and share the load.
You do not have to do this journey alone.

WHAT YOU ARE CREATING IS SO NEEDED

This is a reminder that what you are co-creating is so needed!
The world needs your gifts, your qualities, your creations, your magic.
However they come, whatever form they take.
Keep going. Keep creating. Keep holding the vision.
Even if it feels messy, un-clear, non-linear, all over the place.
Let it be what it is, and remember, deeply remember, and take a moment to breathe this in:

What you are creating is SO needed!

CREATION IN EVERY MOMENT

When you pause for a moment, just long enough to take in what's actually happening around and within you, you'll notice that you are creating in every single moment.

From the words you speak, to the feelings you are feeling, the thoughts you are thinking and the energy you are embodying. Each moment leads on to the next and is a web connecting to each and every part, making up the whole creation of your life.

EMBODIED CREATION SHARE

I sometimes feel so much my heart is almost going to explode out of my chest.
My senses are so alive that the smallest of sensations ripples deeply in my womb.
When I close my eyes I can feel the warmth of the soft wind whispering on my skin.
The sunshine peeking through the clouds delights me with its little bursts of warmth.
Birds, crickets, the cicada of the African climes bring music to my ears.
Being alive is a gift.
Getting to experience what it means to be human in a full-feeling body is a privilege.
As I am invited to connect more deeply with my beautiful, wise, intuitive body, I realise even more deeply how I am creating every moment with my awareness.
I truly can create heaven on Earth in my body.
My home.

THE LATE SUMMER CAULDRON

My womb space is a cauldron of seeds planted, action taken, and nurture given, sprinkled with alignment and a deep vision holding it.

Now is the time to let it bubble and simmer in the later summer sun.

Alchemy is happening.
Magic is brewing.
Just like a watched kettle never boils, this space of creation needs space and time to do its thing.
When the autumn comes, it will be ready for harvest.

Until then.
Rest.
Wait.
Be patient.

Soak up the rays and spend time out in nature.
Let your body bask in the season's end.

It needs this nourishment to sustain it through the winter.
It needs this nourishment to keep on creating.

DEEPEN YOUR CONNECTION

As you co-create with what wants to come through, there will be moments when you simply need to connect with the energy of what you are creating, deeply getting to know it.

Just be with it.
Feel it.
Hear it.
Notice it.
Hold it.

Simply spend time deepening your relationship.
Ask it how it wants to be nourished.
Ask it how it wants you to connect with it.

Treat it like a new love that you are getting to know, and listen attentively as it shares, growing your connection.

EMBODIED CREATION SHARES

'As I connected to the soul of my business, it did not show up straight away. It felt like a new connection that needed nurturing. As I came to the end of the visualisation, I started to feel the energy more solidly, rooted, and it was inviting me to root myself as well as value my work. There was a nudge to release fears and remove my masks … Deepening the connection, I saw myself at the edge of a forest in the dark of the night. There was a faint light that kept calling out to me to "bring my fire". I was shown that what lights me up is what lights my business up. I was invited to bring in the activities that fuel me and light the fire within me.'
Avey

'When I connect with the energy of what's coming through, it's this kind of red dragon energy. It's very powerful. I feel some fear in it, and power, which also feels overpowering at times. At the same time I feel like the dragon is showing me how to make the energy safe for me.'
Sophia

WAITING CAN FEEL LIKE TORTURE

We are so conditioned to be constantly doing. Taking action. Finding a solution. Making things happen.

'If we aren't doing something, are we still being productive?' is a belief that has been ingrained into the threads of modern society. Waiting for the creation to appear, to be made manifest without seemingly doing anything can be one of the hardest things.

It can bring up all the things – thoughts, ideas and beliefs telling you that you should just give up. You aren't enough. It's never going to happen. Things like this don't happen to people like you. What's the point? If you aren't doing something, you may as well forget it.

STOP.

Let those thoughts go. If you need to, take some time to journal on them, hold them, acknowledge them, release them, ask them lovingly to step to one side.

Then, once again tune into the wisdom of your body.
This space of intuitive knowing that creates just by being in existence.

Now is the time to have faith, and to trust.

Deeply.

So much is happening beneath the surface that you may not even be consciously aware of.

Your job for now is to trust in the timing. You will know when it's ready.

YOU ARE UNLIMITED

You are unlimited.
You are filled with creative potential.
You embody all you desire.
You are what you have been looking for all along.

It's time to remember this.
It's time to look inside.
It's time to let yourself be who you truly are.
It's time to unleash your greatness.

AUTUMN/FALL

Yin

Waning moon

Element – Water

Chakras – root, sacral, heart, throat (not limited to these)

Qualities – letting go, releasing, harvesting

THE AUTUMN CROSSOVER

I feel irritated.
I feel angry.
I feel fed up.

There isn't flow. There's a stuckness. A jamming, as though something is blocking the pipes.

I'm tired.
I'm self-critical.
I'm impatient.
Why aren't things happening faster?

What's going on beneath the surface?

I actually feel really tired.
I actually just want to let go.
But if I do I'm afraid nothing will happen.
It will have all been for nothing.
My efforts will go unrewarded.

So I must keep holding on, to feel like I am in control, poised and ready to act on any guidance that I receive.

But, what if, what if, I listen to my body.
What if I truly let go.
Forget about it today.
Do something else.
Be someone else.
Be just me.

As I turn to nature for guidance, this is the time of year when the leaves begin to loosen their grip, release and let go. The winds have changed, bringing cooler air and a stirring up of it all. My stomach certainly feels this energy.

This is the time to surrender it all.
Loosen the grip.
Let the faucet flow.

USE THE POWER OF YOUR VOICE

With all the chaos, uncertainty and whirling that comes up as we rewrite the old, it can feel like everything is falling apart.
Whilst that is not necessarily a bad thing, it can definitely bring up all the things.

Hold them, acknowledge them, feel them, be with them.
Give them what they need.
Lovingly release them.
Or ask Mother Earth to transmute them.

Then come back to the power of your voice.

Declare your intention. Speak it to the Universe.
Ask for help. Speak it to the Universe.
Use your words to ask for what you need to support you right now.

Feel the softening … the letting go … in knowing it is done.

Your words, your voice, carry more power than you have ever been taught.

EMBODIED CREATION PRACTICE

I invite you to feel into and begin to use this alchemical power you hold. Speaking what you desire, intend, or need out loud is so powerful and can create miracles in your life. So many of us have been taught to shut down our voices, to not speak or ask, so I invite you to begin to voice your needs out loud to the Universe. As you do this, notice what it brings up for you.

If you find it hard to connect to the voice, you may want to get some healing support with either the throat and/or sacral chakras, as they are connected. A lot of us have ancestral and personal memories of being silenced, so this is a big area for many. There are some resources at the end to support you in this.

THE CHAOS OF AUTUMN

Let it be messy.
Let it be wild.
Feel it all, moving through your veins and your limbs.

Dance with abandon.
Sway to the rhythm of your lifeforce.

Forget order.
Forget control.
Forget trying to fit in a box.

Cry.
Scream.
Sweat.

Let that wild within come forth.
Let the magic of stars colliding be felt.
Let yourself be taken.
Let yourself be moved.

Let go.
Let go.
Let go.

This season can invite you into the not knowing. It might be messy. You might try to hold on. Figure it out. Control it. The invitation here is to get comfortable with not knowing, with the discomfort of it and anything else rising.

ENDINGS

Creation is as much about endings as it is beginnings. It is the deep honouring of death at the end of a cycle, the letting go, knowing when something is not working and allowing it to fade away, before the rebirth. Allowing the necessary grief to occur, with a side of harvesting and celebration from the gifts it has brought. It is a return to the natural rhythms and cycles of life.

We are so used to taking, wanting more, more, more, for things to never end. We create like crazy, fuelled by feelings of lack and not feeling safe and secure. If we just have this item, more money in the bank, we will be okay.

This has led to a complete imbalance as we live totally out of alignment with our own natural cycles – staying up all hours, working, seeking quick-pleasure-fixes, feeding our insecurities. We rape and pillage from our Great Mother to feed the machine and keep producing.

There's no time for rest, letting go, creating space for the ways and the new that will bring about change. There's no time to stop and actually connect within, to get to the root of what's actually going on inside – what's feeding this constant need to be 'on' in the summer of life. Holding and healing the pains, the ancestral traumas, the conditioning that we have been fed. Stopping to care for one another and connect deeply, remembering we truly are all one.

It's time to make space for endings, for death. To stop fearing it. Instead, lean into its alchemical presence. Letting this natural part of the cycle do its job, stop fighting it, surrender to it, and receive all the gifts, including rebirth and creation, that will in time come from it.

EMBODIED CREATION PROMPTS

- *What are you holding on to?*
- *What is it time to let go of?*
- *What ending/s have you been avoiding?*

- *What support do you need, if any?*

I also invite you to take a moment to acknowledge the gifts you have received from endings, even if at the time they may have been hard.

When we are birthing the new, we often have opportunities to let go, grieve, and hold what never was acknowledged, to clear the way for holding what is coming through. You may also be called to let go of a way of living or being, perhaps an idea or what you thought something was going to look like. Allow yourself to do this, to acknowledge this, and hold space for it.

ARE YOU WILLING?

Are you willing to be different and think differently to the norm?
Are you willing to walk a different path to those around you?
Are you willing to follow the guidance to co-create with the energies?
Are you willing to let everything go that isn't in alignment?
Are you willing to let any beliefs, ideas, conditioning, and stories fall away that aren't supportive?
Are you willing to trust when it's time to let something go and not try anymore?
Are you willing to let things go even if it's difficult, uncomfortable, painful even?
Are you willing to let it be messy?
Are you willing to do what it takes on this path?

EMBODIED CREATION SHARE

Letting go is something I've definitely learned the hard way in the past. When it's come to relationships, homes, friendships and even in offerings, programmes, with clients and my business – I was trying to hold on to things and make them work when I knew inside it wasn't right.

I had to let my first business completely go. I was trying to be a health and wellness coach and it felt like a struggle to me for almost the whole four and a half years I was doing it. I barely made any money and was still working in many other part time jobs. I love health and wellness and the world needs coaches in it, but it was not for me. I felt for a long time that it was more for my personal journey and something I will always include in my life and work, but not something I am here to necessarily do

When I let go of it, (which wasn't easy – I felt like I was failing after all those years, like I'd wasted time and money), I created the space for my current business to come in. It took a few months, but it came – like the most magical download – combining my varied experience and aligning it with the chakras! SO much more potent, exciting, and aligned than I could have ever tried to make happen. All the experience, of course, also wasn't wasted, and I am beyond grateful I let go of what I thought I was supposed to be doing to make space for what wanted to come.

OWN YOUR WHOLENESS

To create a world that benefits the whole, we each have to welcome back in and own our own whole.

The patriarchy thrives on labels, separation, on 'either/or'.
You can't hold both opposites, there are no layers in the middle, nuances or parts.
You are either a saint or a sinner, good or bad, a virgin or a whore.
There's no space for it all to thrive. As what would 'control' do if it can't box you in?

It's time to let it all out.
Stop being defined as one thing and own all of your shades.

Be messy AND put together.
Be sweet and innocent AND wild and passionate.
Be fierce and fiery AND gentle and reflective.
Be a leader AND a supporter.
Be lazy AND a go-getter.
Be a scientist AND an intuitive.
Be a destroyer AND a creator.
Be grounded AND multi-dimensional.
Be masculine AND feminine.
Be all of it.

You aren't just one thing. So stop trying to squeeze and define yourself in a singular way. As you shut down your parts they become illnesses, caged wild animals longing for freedom, trapped emotions that morph into resentment, hostility and rage.

They need space to breathe. To be heard and be felt. Be lived through you as an all-encompassing-dynamic human.

Then they aren't nearly as scary as they have been made out to be.

As you let yourself expand, be undefined, be YOU, you create a ripple of wholeness that jumps from one person to the next.

Saying it's okay to be fully you.

As you welcome in and own ALL of you, you birth a new possibility which only comes from this union.

We need ALL of you.

EMBODIED CREATION SHARE

Sapi was going through a really tough time when we were connecting. Her close family member was very sick, and it was incredibly emotional and draining. She was being called to bring through more joy into her life, and in general through her creations. As she spent time connecting to this energy, feeling it in her body, she found she was crying a lot. It felt both extremely cathartic, like her body needed to release a lot of emotion, also there was happiness in connecting to the future, which took her beyond her current circumstances.

Sometimes, as we allow what wants to come through, we find ourselves holding the duality of life. I invite you to let yourself be here.

EMBODIED CREATION PROMPT

• *Where can you embody your duality and begin to own it more?*

Welcoming All of You

What are the parts that you have shut down or not acknowledged?

It's about accepting, welcoming, integrating, reclaiming and embodying them.
Holding them so they support you. Bringing you into wholeness.

My part is my wild, earthy, Goddess energy. She is bold. She knows. She just is.
There's a sexual energy she embodies which used to scare me as it felt unwelcome.
It's my creative power. My creative essence.
It's the part of me that creates through pleasure.
I always felt it, knew it was there – but I felt ashamed of it.
So I shut her down, I tried to bury her deep.

But over time she began to squeeze through the gaps.
In moments of alcohol and drug-fuelled frenzies.
She leaked into spaces when I was carefree and surrendered.
Finding a way to be embodied that became destructive.
Causing chaos as she wouldn't be silenced.

She needed to be acknowledged and honoured.
Revered for her fierce, bold and creative power.
Embodied in a way that was rooted, grounded and held.

Embodied Creation Prompts

* *What is/are the part/s that you have shut down?*
* *What support do they need?*
* *How do they need to be held to truly be felt and embodied?*

HARVESTING AND OFFERING

As the energy draws inwards, there's a call to go within. An innate knowing that signals rest is coming soon.
It's time to reap the rewards of the seeds that have been planted.
It's time to collect and gather, to pluck the ripe fruits and harvest the gifts.

Perhaps there's some inspired action that can be taken to bring in your desire. Letting the last of the waning yang current carry you through.
Maybe it's time to take stock of where things are and see what needs to stay and what needs to go.

Also remember to keep regularly tending to the fire, the energy of creation – keeping it stoked and lit, its embers glowing, magnetising your desire towards you.
Holding that grounded space ready for it to come into the physical.

And as you harvest and bring in, I invite you to offer thanks to all those around you – seen and unseen – that have been a part of your support team and holding.
Honour the journey, the process, the unfolding of it and what it's taken to get to here.
Share the gifts of your bounty and all that you have received.
Give back to Mama Earth, thanking her for holding you.

WINTER

Yin

New/dark moon

Element – Earth

Chakras – Earth star, root, sacral (not limited to these)

Qualities – rest, nourishment, grounding, space

THE WISDOM OF THE MENSTRUAL WINTER

The first day of my bleed was a time I used to dread every month, especially in my teens and twenties. Knowing I would be in agony, waves of cramps rolling out from my womb space. I was living and working the 'normal' way then. Having to push through and get things done, no matter what my body was telling me.

Today, through consciously creating my life to be on my terms, I get to choose and create my days, and I am so deeply grateful.

This time in my cycle is now one of my favourites. It's my most potent, connected and deep part. My intuition is at its peak, I have an attitude of no bullshit (which I love more and more, the older I get), and that feeling of needing to burst that comes with the end of the autumn/fall part has released. There's flow, there's movement, there's a letting go and shedding happening.

I am being called to rest more now. To nourish my body in a gentle and replenishing way. There's no pushing here, and those that I do connect with will get the part of me that is quieter, more inward, less smiley, and I will get straight to the point. There's no space for entertaining, as I know my cave is calling to lean into the deep wisdom of my inner winter.

EMBODIED CREATION PRACTICE

I invite you to tune into your menstrual winter, the dark/new moon, or the middle of winter seasonally where you live, whichever one appeals to you.

How do you feel about this time seasonally/cyclically? I invite you to let yourself surrender into this energy of darkness without an agenda or purpose. What comes up for you?

ⒹEEP ROOTS

Roots grow as we tend to ourselves.
We deal with the things that rise.
We sit with them.
We hold them.
We give them what they need.

Every time you hold space for yourself and allow yourself to let go, to grieve, to release in some way, or to simply be where you are at, you clear the space for your roots to bury down a little deeper.

We need strong, deep foundations upon which to grow the creations needed to weather it all. To be the change the world needs. To withstand the test of time. To spread their seeds through many seasons and bring about the Earth our hearts are calling for.

EMBODIED CREATION PRACTICE

I invite you to write a letter to your creation as though you would a dear friend or family member. Ask whatever you would like to know. Ask for it to share with you what it needs, and perhaps what you need to support it. Ask whatever you would like. Or simply begin 'Dear xxx, what would you like to share with me today?'

SlowDown

slow   down

Dream on it

Pay attention to your dreams.
Let them guide you.
Let them whisper to you.
The dreamscape is a place of magic, possibility, and potential.

If you need guidance and aren't receiving it (that could be guidance in itself), perhaps you could take it to your dreams.

If you are calling for a way forward, a way not yet a reality, take it to your dreams.

If you need help in any way, I invite you to dream on it.

Embodied Creation Practice

Set an intention before going to sleep to receive what you need in your dreams. Upon waking, before doing anything, I invite you to note down your dreams. Look for signs, feelings, meanings – anything that might support you. You might need to do this for a while, and trust the answers are coming.

SELF-CARE IS A HUGE PART OF THIS JOURNEY

This is the part I see people resist and leave out the most. We have been so conditioned to think if we are not being productive, nothing is happening. We're missing out, we're not going to get where we want to be.

But the way I see it is that you are the vessel for holding what wants to come through you. What I have realised deeply with myself and clients is that often we are first called into this next level of wellness for ourselves. We have to deeply look after our bodies (mind and soul) so that they can hold what wants to come. It may not come to you if you can't hold it. You need to be ready for it.

This can take the form of basic nourishment – eating fresh food, moving daily, getting into nature, grounding, etc. It's ensuring you are filled up – overflowing, even – and able to hold the energy.

If you would like to read more of my journey around this as well as receive 52 self-care actions, guidance and ideas that I use to this day, I invite you to check out my book *Embodied*. Details are in the resources section at the end.

EMBODIED CREATION SHARES

Message from connecting to the soul of a business: 'What's important is that we work together to make a bigger difference, in a smarter way that keeps you well, strong and healthy. I can help you to stay well. Just stay connected and listen. This really isn't as hard as you're making it. It doesn't have to be perfect either. You've done all the hard work getting to this point, laying the foundations and building the reputation and credentials. I can't manifest if you are not well, healthy and energised, so it's in both of our interests for you to be so, it can be a shared commitment.'
Grace Rose

Conversation with Sophia:
'I'm being called to create space to deeply nourish, and at the same

time, I can feel this division in the whole. I can feel my body wants to rest and my head wants to jump ahead. It feels as if the head can only relax when it knows what's going to come and that it's going to be okay. The body trusts already, and I can feel this fight between the body and the head, as my head tries to justify not doing anything.'

'Where does it come from?' I asked.

'It's definitely a conditioning. I see my parents in their mid-70s still needing to get up at 8 o'clock and do things. There's this need to always be productive.'

We went into it further, feeling this energy, what colour it had. It was red which has connotations around survival and the Catholic church. It felt like a connection to 'being the good girl, of having to do well, contribute by doing to be accepted, to be loved and to belong. You can't put your needs first, you're not allowed to put your body's needs first.'

We explored it a bit further, and this belief had been passed down Sophia's female ancestral line, and it felt like something she was still carrying that she knew it was time to let go of.
It felt intuitively that the Goddess Mary Magdalene was an energy to invoke and work with, as an embodiment of love, sensuality and pleasure. To allow herself to connect deeply with her own needs and honour her body as part of the Divine. To start connecting with the colour red and re-claiming it as a part of her physical body and begin to feel its safety and holding. To feel like she isn't alone on this journey, even though she may be carrying the beliefs from many in her lineage. It's time to start remembering the power of the Divine Feminine, and its gifts.

EMBODIED CREATION PRACTICE
As we begin to create with our bodies and the power of the feminine way, we can lean on the support of the unseen. Many of the ancient teachings which honoured the feminine way have been lost or changed to adopt a different meaning which suited the patriarchy. If you are called to this way, you can connect to the wisdom you hold within, call on the unseen support and let it guide you. There are also resources available, and as you ask for this support trust the ones that fall into

your path.

Which Goddesses or Gods are present in your life right now and what energies do they embody for you? If this is new for you, I invite you to set an intention for a quality you want to embody and allow the deity to come and make themself known to you.

NOTHING, BUT SO MUCH

Sometimes there's nothing.

My body feels heavy, tired. It's telling me no. Stop. Don't push on or force anything.

I try to take action. I try to do something. Anything. To feel productive. To feel like I am moving forward.

Then that 'tired but wired' feeling creeps upon me. 'If you don't listen, I'll get louder.'
It turns into a wall.
My body is letting me know.

Now is the time to rest. To listen. To be.

Still.

Trusting that when the time is right, the guidance will come.

But for now, I am being asked to be with this. Fully.

Under the surface, cells are replenishing. Ideas are being alchemised. Deep magic is rumbling. Transformation is happening. And when the wheel turns and the stars align, it will make itself known.

Until then.

Rest. Patience.

EMBODIED CREATION SHARE

'The dominant feeling and message I get when connecting with the soul of my business is stillness and silence – not the absence of sound, but the absence of noise. It feels deeply peaceful.'
May

CREATING FROM THE VOID

Breathe into your body.
Notice the areas of tightness, tension, where you are holding on.
Breathe into them and let them soften a little bit more.
Notice what's going on in your mind, notice where you are trying to escape, be busy, rush off.

With each breath let your body relax into the holding from beneath.
Let it be heavy.
Let it be supported.
Stop holding on so tightly.

Feel the way your body breathes itself.
The rise and fall of your belly.
Breath making its way into your fingers and toes.
Nourishing air coming in.
Breathing away what no longer serves.

Let the breath create space in your body.
Pockets of emptiness like jewels studded all over.
Creating an expansion, an ease, an allowing.
Let yourself melt into this opening.

This space of possibility.
Space to create sustainably.
Space to feel the vibration of the new.
Space to welcome in what you deeply desire.
Space that feels damn good in your body.

Breathe it in.
Deeply.

Just be with it.

THE SPACE IN BETWEEN

There's a space in between.
That's not one thing or another.
It's liminal.
Empty.

Don't fill it up.
Sit with it.
Be with it.
Feel its edges.

It's where Universes are born from.
Creations seed themselves.
It's a space of integration and rest.
It's deeply important.
I invite you to honour it.

In time it is where the guidance will come.
Where you will hear those whispers.
Where you can feel what's aligned for YOU.
Where your soul has space to connect with you.

EMBODIED CREATION PROMPTS

- *Where can you create more space in your life?*
- *How can you honour the space in between?*

EMBODIED CREATION SHARE

One of my mentors – who is also a friend – was guided to take 16 months out of her business, not working. She was waking every day with anxiety, unsure where the money would come from. But throughout, her guidance was telling her to wait, hold, be, not take action, and she was supported. Then one day as she was doing her daily journaling, out of nowhere she suddenly received the whole programme, outline and offer for what she shares today, and it has gone on to become a six-figure business supporting women to do similar as she had to go through.

I deeply acknowledge how hard this can be and it takes enormous amounts of trust and faith. Sometimes we may need to do something else to support ourselves whilst we create the space for things to re-align, taking the pressure off.

WHAT SUPPORT DO YOU NEED?

Your job is to keep supporting yourself to hold what wants to come through.

To be able to receive it.
To be able to connect with it.
To be able to ground it.
To be able to support it.

To share it if that's what is called.
To take action if needed.
To be its physical counterpart.
To co-create with it.

We all need holding in the physical to bring forward the most potent, deep, and magical creations.

It could be someone to look after your children.
Someone to support you with nourishment and just be there as a presence supporting you.
Someone to guide you and mentor you.
Someone to hold space for you.
Someone to believe in you.
Someone who just gets it!

EMBODIED CREATION PROMPTS

* *Who is holding you as you hold space for what wants to come through?*
* *What support do you need?*

Birthing Your Creation

This section includes some guidance and support for birthing your creation into the physical. This way of creating and bringing in the new can bring up a lot, so there's also some support around fears that can rise.

FEARS AROUND BIRTHING WHAT WANTS TO COME

There may be very real fears around birthing the new.
Allowing creations of ancient yet modern wisdom through.

There were times when these gifts were seen as witchcraft, sorcery, evil.
Bearers and midwives of them burned at the stake.
Communities, healers, tribes, banished and wiped out.
Still to this day, people can mysteriously 'disappear'.
For sharing the truth, their wisdom and leading from the heart.

The patriarchy came in with its systems of oppression.
Its need to put everything away that can't be quantified.
Its need for control and having to be right.
Its need to keep feeding that bottom line.

All that goes against this, feels at risk.
Even writing these words triggers deep waves of fear.

But you have to keep going.
The world needs what's coming through.

Seek out communities and others who get it.
Do what you can to hold and acknowledge the fears.
Get support where you need it.
Look after yourself.

Lean into our ancient Earth Mother.
Feel her grounding and support.
Let her hold you.
Find safety in her womb.

Know it won't be in vain.
You are here to birth the new.

I honour you and I thank you for your bravery and your courage.
I honour you for walking this path and for being you.

EMBODIED CREATION SHARE

At the end stages of writing this book, I began experiencing a lot of that 'wired but tired' feeling, specifically in my arms, shoulders and upper back. It was strange as it was just confined to that area, and no amount of stretching, yin yoga, meditating, or self-massage was shifting it. It was getting progressively stronger, and I was beginning to feel threads of fear in it. It felt very confusing and was beginning to overwhelm me.

So, I started to deeply connect with this part of my body, letting it speak to me, letting it guide me. What came up was an energy that felt ancestral, past life-y and collective around being safe. The words I kept getting were 'It's not safe to be you. It's not safe to create foundations or receive for your work as it will just be taken away anyway. It doesn't matter what your intention is, they will be out to get you.'

For this situation, I decided to tap (using EFT) through the emotions, allowing them to share and express with me, then to be released from my body.

As I did, the fear rising felt so real at one point I was literally shaking and had tears streaming as my body remembered all the times (merged together) where it wasn't safe to share things outside of the norm, like past-life regressions or co-creating with energies. You had to fear for your life and be ready to move or run in an instant just for helping people. Or you could get thrown in jail or have legal battles.

Much of my life has felt very unstable and like it's happening to me, with being adopted, family changes, etc. Even now, at the time of writing, I don't have a home and have moved house over 15 times in the past 22 years. There was definitely a connection to feeling safe to root, ground, and lay physical foundations, which ties into being able to hold what wants to come through.

After the tapping, I felt safer and more grounded. It's still something that I will actively work on, as it's a big area for me in my life in general, as it is for many sensitive souls too. But, it feels lighter now, the wired feeling has softened, and there's movement, which is always a step in the right direction.

EMBODIED CREATION PROMPTS

How do you feel about bringing through what wants to come? Are there any fears rising? I invite you to hold space for them, connect with them, and ask them to let you know where they are coming from and what they need. If you need support with this, please reach out to someone you trust. There are some resources at the back also.

IT'S TIME TO BIRTH

Birthing embodied creations can feel like the most difficult and frustrating thing in the world.
They can be I-N-T-E-N-S-E.
They can be all-consuming.
They need your energy and devotion.

You'll want someone else to do it for you.
You may wonder why the hell you said yes to this.
You'll want to give up.

They need you to be fully embodied.
To be fully present.
Keep landing in your body.
Keep being in your body.

Look after your vessel in the most potent way.
Keep nourishing yourself.
Caring for yourself.
Holding yourself.
Resting.
Breathing.

Keep trusting.
Keep showing up.
Keep taking that next little step.

It will soon be here.
You have got this!

ROOTING INTO THE PHYSICAL

The time has come to feel the energy of what you are bringing through fully landing in the physical. This will support the birthing process and allow you to let go of what you have created, knowing it is held and grounded.

EMBODIED CREATION SHARE

As I was coming close to completing Embodied Creation, I felt her energy swirling around my body in a vortex of colours, specifically pink and orange. She then entered my throat and heart, swooping down to my base chakra, through to the Earth. She began to spread her roots far and wide, anchoring into the physical.

Then her trunk began to grow up my body, through my crown chakra and her branches spread out like a canopy around the globe.

This is where she stayed and is firmly embodied, always connected to me, as I release her out into the world.

EMBODIED CREATION PRACTICE

See the energy of your creation birthing into Mother Earth. Ask Mother Earth to support you if needed, and feel your creation here, landed, grounded.

LET IT BE

Release your creation.
Let it be in the world.
It has its own path now.

It will call on you when it needs.
Check in on it like a loving parent.
Support it and share it as asked and guided.
Send it love and hold it in your heart.
See it reaching and connecting with the people who need and want
it.

Know that it has a life of its own.
I invite you to trust this.

A PRAYER/RITUAL FOR RELEASING YOUR CREATION

As your creation makes its way out into the word (physical babies being the exception – although there's no harm in doing the same for them too), you might want to honour it in some way with a ritual and/or prayer.

I invite you to feel into whatever feels aligned and good between you and your creation for this. Trust yourself and your creation – you will know what feels good to do.

As an example, to release *Embodied Creation* I connected with the elements. I burned all the draft copies in a fire and connected with the energy as she transformed into ash and smoke, which made its way into the world. I gave thanks to Mother Earth for her holding and guidance throughout. I picked some oracle cards to send her off with love. Lastly, I bathed in a Colour Mirrors bottle which was tied to the numerology of her name.

Here is a prayer I wrote for *Embodied Creation*.

Dear *Embodied Creation*,

Thank you for our journey.
Thank you for holding me.
Thank you for all you have given me.
You have transformed me.
I am a different person to the one who began when we first connected.

You have challenged me.
You have stretched me.
Grown me and filled me up.

It has been my greatest honour to bring you through and receive the gifts of your journey.
I am always here for you, and I feel a silver thread connecting us

always.

Now I release you into the world, to reach, support, and connect to those that are calling for you.

All my love,
Tara

REST, INTEGRATE AND CELEBRATE

After the birthing, take time to rest and integrate. Take as long as you need, let your body guide you. As you give it this time and space to land, you will likely receive more from it, as creations that are birthed in this way have a habit of giving back. So also let yourself receive from this essential part of the process.

Finally, I invite you to celebrate yourself and your creation. The part you played in co-creating it, taking it on, allowing it to transform you, work with you, work *through* you.

You are incredible and I honour you for choosing (or perhaps surrendering to) this way.

It's time to celebrate your creation. It's time to celebrate you.

RESOURCES AND WAYS TO SUPPORT YOU ON YOUR JOURNEY OF CO-CREATION

RESOURCES AND WAYS TO SUPPORT YOU ON YOUR JOURNEY OF CO-CREATION

You can access everything here:
https://empathpreneurs.org/resources

Next steps

If you would like to take your journey of embodied creation further, I invite you to check out my programme 'Embodied Creation', where I will guide you to connect with Gaia and what is calling to come through you at this time, taking the steps to bring it into the physical, with your body, the seasons and cycles. I will be supporting you with any healing and holding to embody who you are being called into, with a supportive community alongside.

Additional resources and support from me

Access your free visualisations mentioned in the book here:
- Connect with your heart visualisation
- Connecting to feminine power
- Co-creating with Gaia
- Connecting with what wants to come through
- Magnetising your vision

Co-create with the soul of your business

Three visualisations to connect to the essence and life-force of your business, so that you can co-create with it.

Create just for you

A date to create – an online held space to tune into your creative centres and body and create just for you.

My books (available anywhere you buy your books online):

Embodied – A self-care guide for sensitive souls.
Embodied Business – A guide to grounding and aligning your business chakras for 'empathpreneurs'.

Oracle card deck

Embodied Wisdom – Colour alchemy card deck to guide you into alignment with your truth.

Programmes, workshops and courses:

Business Chakras Alchemy – an 11-week course (with access for the lifetime of it, including all updates), to clear, heal and release chakras blocks that might be holding you back in some way.

Embodied Business – a 12-month membership space for 'empathpreneurs' to co-create with their businesses, create aligned offers and ground this in the world in a practical way.

Connect and Create with Your Inner Child – a two-part workshop to connect and create with younger versions of yourself.

A Journey Through the Chakras – healing meditations, prompts and tools to support you with each of the chakras: Earth star, root/base, sacral, solar, heart, throat, third eye, crown and soul star.

Suggestions for Ways to Consciously Give Back as a Co-Creator on Earth

'Do the best you can until you know better. Then when you know better, do better.'
Maya Angelou

Do your inner work to heal and support yourself. When you come from here, you give to others from an empowered, whole place.

Share your wisdom and knowledge with others.

Learn from others, find out what's going on in the world, especially in the areas you are being called to create change. Many sensitive souls avoid this (I have done too), as it can feel overwhelming. Also, in spiritual circles, we are often taught you'll attract more of it if you bring your attention to it – but this often comes from a place of privilege, and you need to have some awareness of what's going on already to spark and create change, in my opinion!

Give consciously to organisations and individuals you believe in who look to empower others. I recommend doing your research here as it is often the smaller, on-the-ground ones that have the quickest, most effective impact to a specific situation.

Know where your money goes. Choose to spend your money on products/services/items which are ethical, fair, local, eco-conscious and support others. As long as we support services which employ cheap labour, are un-ethical and adopt unfair practices, the longer they stay alive.

Be a kind and considerate human being. Tap into that huge heart of yours and offer support when you see, feel or know it is needed.

Give your time.

Share about organisations and businesses you believe in on your social feeds and with friends and family.

MORE BOOKS AND RESOURCES

The power and beauty of the body

Code Red, by Lisa Lister
The Joyous Body, by Clarissa Pinkola Estés
Wild Power: Discover the Magic of Your Menstrual Cycle, by Alexandra Pope and Sjanie Hugo Wurlitzer

Inspiration from nature

Braiding Sweetgrass, by Robin Wall Kimmerer
Mysteries of the Dark Moon, by Demetra George
Moonology, by Yasmin Boland
The Enchanted Life, by Sharon Blackie
The Hidden Life of Trees, by Peter Wohlleben
The Hidden Messages in Water, by Masaru Emoto
Speaking with Nature, by Sandra Ingerman and Llyn Roberts

The Goddess, feminine, and mothers

Awakening to Kali, by Sally Kempton
Burning Woman, by Lucy H. Pearce
Mary Magdalene Revealed, by Meggan Waterson
Rise Sister Rise, by Rebecca Campbell
The Way of the Priestess, by Dr Sarah Coxon
Unbound, by Nicola Humber
Untamed, by Glennon Doyle
Wild Mercy, by Mirabai Starr
Womb Awakening, by Azra and Seren Bertrand
Women's Wisdom from the Heart of Africa, by Sobonfu Somé
You are a Goddess, by Sophie Bashford

Pleasure and sexuality

Desire Lines, by Anna Sansom
In Touch with Yourself – a Course, by Anna Sansom and Jennie Verleg
Mama Gena's School of Womanly Arts: Using the Power of Pleasure to Have Your Way with the World, by Regena Thomashauer
Pussy: A Reclamation, by Regena Tomashauer

Healing and holding

Advanced Energy Anatomy, by Carolin Myss
Deep Liberation: Shamanic Tools for Reclaiming Wholeness in a Culture of Trauma, by Langston Kahn
Dying to be Me, by Anita Moorjani
Home Coming: Reclaiming and Championing Your Inner Child, by John Bradshaw
In the Realm of Hungry Ghosts: Close Encounters with Addiction, by Dr. Gabor Maté
It Didn't Start With You, by Mark Wolynn
Many Lives, Many Masters, by Brian Weiss
Me and White Supremacy, by Layla F Saad
Radical Self-Love, by Gala Darling
Rosa's Choice, Healing the wounds of the mother, by Debra Kilby
The Body Keeps the Score, by Bessel van der Kolk
The Energy Codes, by Dr Sue Morter
The Power of Voice, by Denise Morter
The Shadow King, by Sidra Stone

Creativity

Big Magic, by Liz Gilbert
Creatrix – She Who Makes, by Lucy H. Pearce
The Artist's Way, by Julia Cameron
The Creative Doer, by Anna Lovind
The Creative Fire, by Clarissa Pinkola Estés

Manifesting and creating

Ask and It Is Given, by Esther and Jerry Hicks
Creative Visualization, by Shakti Gawain
Get Rich, Lucky Bitch, by Denise Duffield Thomas
It's Not Your Money, by Tosha Silver
Money Manifestation Mastery, by Lara Waldman
Rich as F*ck, by Amanda Frances
The Complete Works of Florence Scovel Shinn, by Florence Scovel Shinn
The Secret, by Rhonda Byrne
The Soul of Money, by Lynne Twist
Think and Grow Rich, by Napoleon Hill

Think Yourself Rich, by Anthony Norvell
You Are a Badass at Making Money, by Jen Sincero

Documentaries

A Plastic Ocean – the plastic pollution in the world's oceans.
Brave Blue World: Racing to Solve Our Water Crisis
Cowspiracy: The Sustainability Secret
Earthlings – humans' reliance on animals for economic purposes.
Fantastic Fungi – the magic and beauty of the mushroom world.
Minimalism: A Documentary About the Important Things
My Octopus Teacher – a female octopus who captivates a filmmaker off the coast of South Africa.
The *Blue Planet* collection – David Attenborough's series on the beauty of our planet.
The True Cost – who pays the real price for your clothes.
What the Health – the link between diet and disease and the billions at stake in the industries that promote it.

ACKNOWLEDGEMENTS

The biggest thank you to the magical humans around the globe who have all contributed to this book, even if our conversations did not make the final pages. Your honesty, vulnerability, hearts, and time have meant the world to me, and you were integral to the stages this book went through to get to what it has become. All the love and gratitude dear Will, Santina, Kasia, Nitin, Lulu, Dani, Ngosa, Saagar, Georgie and Jnana Dev.

My dearest Karin, thank you for walking this path alongside me. Thank you for believing in me, having faith in me and letting me share this 'way' with you, and deeply embodying it. Having your support, love, and incredible journey of creation (as a confirmation and such magic) has kept me going. I am humbled by your wisdom and so happy that we are on this journey together.

Dear Nicola, thank you for being such a powerful space holder and guide throughout, as always. I couldn't have done this without you. You held space for *Embodied Creation* and I, and saw her, even before I could. You and your spaces have changed my life and enabled me to fully step into this way of creating and being. I am forever grateful.

The hugest thank you to the incredible Unbound Press team, especially Lynda and Jesse for your design magic and editing expertise.

Kathryn, I am beyond grateful for our friendship and to you for all of your support. You have held me to go deeper into my own healing and enriched my life on so many levels! I will also be forever grateful that you brought Colour Mirrors into my life.

Thank you Debra for your guidance and holding – especially when I was feeling all the visibility stuff rising! Thank you so much, Moriah, for being a sounding board and grounding when the creation process was 'being messy' ;-) and I couldn't see my way through! I am truly grateful to you both.

Lara, you are a constant inspiration to me and embody this way so deeply. I am truly honoured to know and have you in my life.

Emily, thank you for being such a powerful leader of the new Earth. You inspire me greatly and make me want to do and be better daily. Thank you for your time and wisdom, I am honoured to walk this path alongside you.

Shannon, our collaborations and friendship mean the absolute world to me. Being able to have someone to share this journey with and hold space with has been life-changing for me.

Meron, thank you for all your encouragement and support always, and for being on the phone with me during my butterfly moment. That was truly special!

The hugest thank you to Gigi, Hannah, Julia, Ami, Aaron and Brendan, who support me with my business. You are all incredible and I am so grateful to have you working with me to bring my visions to life.

Thank you to the gorgeous souls who generously gave their time to be early reviewers: Aparna, Anna, Rosalie, Toni, Debra, Angel, Will, Karin, Dani and Lisa. Your feedback and encouragement have meant so much to me and *Embodied Creation*.

Thank you to everyone who has participated in my 'Co-create with the soul of your business' experiences. You have affirmed to me the power of creation in this way and enriched my experience of it. Thank you especially to Toni, Aparna, and Lisa for letting me use some of your shares.

Thank you to my Embodied Business group, I love you all so much. Thank you for being such wonderfully magical souls, who see my vision and let me share and show up and do things in this different way.

To all of my clients, mentors, teachers and friends – you inspire me so much. Thank you.

Last but not least, my family, my biggest supporters from the beginning, love you and thank you all, always!

ḞUTHOR BIO

Tara is an intuitive business mentor, holistic wellbeing coach, artist and author who supports empathpreneurs with releasing, healing and letting go of all that is stopping them from fully claiming their magic and co-creating the business (and life) of their dreams that considers all and our home.

She is the author of *Embodied – A Self-Care Guide for Sensitive Souls* and *Embodied Business – A Guide to Grounding and Aligning Your Business Chakras for Empathpreneurs*, and the *Embodied Wisdom* oracle card deck, all published with The Unbound Press.

Find her at www.empathpreneurs.org.

Lightning Source UK Ltd.
Milton Keynes UK
UKHW021153230522
403388UK00014B/780